Ecological Messages in Indian Children's Literature: Conversations with the Creators

Shobha Ramaswamy

Ukiyoto Publishing

All global publishing rights are held by

Ukiyoto Publishing

Published in 2024

Content Copyright ©Shobha Ramaswamy

ISBN 9789361725906

All rights reserved.
No part of this publication may be reproduced, transmitted, or stored in a retrieval system, in any form by any means, electronic, mechanical, photocopying, recording or otherwise, without the prior permission of the publisher.

The moral rights of the author have been asserted.

This book is sold subject to the condition that it shall not by way of trade or otherwise, be lent, resold, hired out or otherwise circulated, without the publisher's prior consent, in any form of binding or cover other than that in which it is published.

www.ukiyoto.com

Dedication

My sincere thanks to The University Grants Commission, New Delhi and to all the wonderful people who generously shared their enthusiasm for inculcating ecological messages to children and young adults

Author's Note

Indian writing in English for children and young adults has come of age, with a plethora of talented and dedicated writers contributing their creative efforts towards the growth of this new field.

From the re-telling of folk tales, mythological stories and classics such as the Panchatantra, Hitopadesha and the Jataka Tales, Indian writing for the young passed through a phase of western influence and has now emerged with a voice of its own.

Indian fiction in English for children and young adults is realistic and deals with the problems and interest of the day. It is neither sentimental nor overtly didactic, but has attained the golden mean. Humour and fantasy, too, have their place, as do mystery and adventure stories, tales of the supernatural, science fiction and historical and mythological creative fiction. Writers for the young have also shown their concern for ecology and the natural environment.

Prominent writers include Nilima Sinha, Ranjit Lal, Deepak Dalal, Ira Saxena, Paro Anand, Devika Rangachari, Anushka Ravishankar, Asha Nehemiah, Monideepa Sahu, Payal Dhar, Zai Whitaker, Harini Gopalswami Sreenivasan, Vandana Singh, Suniti Namjoshi,and Deepa Agarwal, among others. Writers such as Anita Desai, Chitra Banerjee Divakaruni, Anita Nair, Mahaswetha Devi and Sashi Deshpande have also written for the young.

Apart from long-established publishers such as Children's Book Trust and National Book Trust, highly innovative publishing houses such as Tulika, Tara, Katha, Pratham Books, Karadi Tales, Terrapin, Red Turtle, Young Zubaan , Duckbill and India Ink, to name a few, have emerged successfully.

More academic interest in this burgeoning field which has immense possibilities for fresh research is the need of the hour. This collection of research papers is a humble effort towards this worthy end.

Contents

Meeting the Authors	1
NILIMA SINHA	2
DR.IRA SAXENA	7
SHAMIM PADAMSEE	12
SHOBHA THAROOR SRINIVASAN	14
BENITA SEN	18
DEEPAK DALAL	26
ZAI WHITAKER	30
RANJIT LAL	38
LEELA GOUR BROOME	40
SANDHYA RAO	51
KEN SPILLMAN, Australia	59
ASHA NEHEMIAH	68
HARINI GOPALSWAMI SREENIVASAN	70
RADHA H.S	75
SOWMYA RAJENDRAN	77
NIVEDITHA SUBRAMANIAM	81
D.RONALD HADRIAN	83
Views of the Illustrators	86
MAYA RAMASWAMY	93
PRIYA KURIYAN	95
VANDANA BIST	99
JANUKA DESHPANDE	102
What the Editors and Publishers Have to Say	110
Himanshi Sharma, TERI Books, New Delhi	111
TARA BOOKS	114
MALA KUMAR, CHILDRENS' AUTHOR AND PUBLISHER OF PRATHAM BOOKS, BANGALORE	118
Interview with Saraswathy Rajagopalan, Editor, Mango Books, Kochi	121
SHOBHA VISWANATH –PUBLISHING DIRECTOR AND CO-FOUNDER, KARADI TALES, CHENNAI	128
Dr.MINI KRISHNAN	131
INTERVIEW WITH SANDHYA RAO, former Editor, Tulika Books, Chennai	134
Some Suggestions from Environmentalists	138
Interview with Payal B. Molur, Wildlife Educator, Bangalore	139

INTERVIEW WITH 'OSAI'KALIDAS, Coimbatore-based environmentalist
146
About the Author 149

Meeting the Authors

NILIMA SINHA

Nilima Sinha is one of the best known children's authors of mystery-adventurestories. Her published books include *The Chandipur Jewels*, *Vanishing Trick at Chandipur*, *Adventure on the Golden Lake* and *SOS From Munia* – all prize-winners for Best Fiction. Her *Adventure Before Midnight* was selected for the White Raven List for libraries internationally.*Myster yof the Falling Mountains* is another popular novel written by her. Her Young Adult novel, *Red Blooms in the Forest*,has been critically acclaimed.

She has also written a variety of fiction, including historical fiction, fantasy,countless short stories, plays and biographies. Her other notable books are *The Yellow Butterfly, So Can I, Rishabh in the Land of the Flying Magicians* andfour books in *the Save the Earth Series*. Many of her titles are included in the curriculum in schools.

As translator, editor, researcher and storyteller, Nilima Sinha has been an active member of the Association of Writers and Illustrators for Children (AWIC), the Indian Section of the International Board on Books for Young People (IBBY). She was Vice-President, IBBY and is presently President, AWIC.

Mrs. Sinha: As you know, we are the Indian Section of The International Board of Books for Young People and it was started by a lady called Jella Lepman, who was Swiss, after the last world war. There was a lot of devastation and she found that children were in a very bad state and she found that stories helped children. So she started collecting books from all over the world for the children who were at camps. A lot of children who had escaped from Jewish camps, from German camps. She started giving them books. She found that it helped them a lot.

Me: Readingtherapy.

Mrs.Sinha: Yes, reading therapy. It was a kind of reading therapy and that was how she got this idea of forming this organisation. It soon had branches all over the world and they tried to help children through books. That was the main idea and now we have so many, many countries who are part of IBBY. We (The Association of Writers and Illustrators for Children) are also part of IBBY and we are working towards promoting the habit of reading- trying to get good books for children and through story-telling and other activities we try to develop the reading habit. But there is still much to be done.

Me: Does fiction play a vital role in a child's life?

Mrs.Sinha: Yes. Of course it is quite natural that fiction will play a vital role becausechildren like to read them. They get entertained, they enjoy reading and specially if it is mystery-adventure stories, (that is what I do). I write mystery-adventure stories as you know.. . . Yes and through the stories they imbibe values. Whatever you want to tell them througha good story which children will enjoy. It becomes more ingrained in their minds if it isthrough a good entertaining story, rather than giving it through non-fiction or trying to givelessons or something they will forget them. They might remember them also, but it goe sinside them moredeeply if it is told through a story.

Me: Can you tell me what you feel about the role of fiction in inculcating ecological values?

Mrs. Sinha: Since you are talking about the environment rather than about moral values . . .
Environment- of course there are a lot of stories in our folktales, Indian traditional folklore. There are stories in them where there is always something or the other about trees, animals.

Through these stories I think children get to know about nature. Yes, people come to love their natural environment, to appreciate it because of this folklore tradition. And as you know in many Indian households, in some areas people worship trees and plants like tulsi and people do puja. So all that is a part of the environment. The environment is taken care of.

Me: Do your books reflect nature and ecological issues? Please share with me your experiences as a writer who portrays nature in her works.

Mrs.Sinha: I know I have written many stories about the environment. I don't know what you would call my experience. It is just that really, when I go to Jharkhand,(that is where my husband's constituency is), it is a very beautiful area. And when we used to go there earlier, it used to be very green and very beautiful and very lush and when we went there after many years, we found that it is all very much depleted degraded. That beauty is gone.

Me: It has become industrialised?

Mrs.Sinha: Industries and very many houses. There is a lot of depletion. So I really feel very bad about it and I have been writing something about vanishing of the forests.

Me: *The Mystery of the Falling Mountains*?

Mrs.Sinha: That is in Himachal Pradesh, in the Himalayan mountains, not in the Jharkhand area. It shows the exploitation of the forest and in fact one of the three main actions of man which has depleted the forests and spoiled the environment, of course, cutting down of trees. The other is mining. And there is something else that I had thought of in that book which I had written about with mountains, I think, cutting down trees and too much building up of resorts, cutting roads through the mountains. Animals also vanish because of that. What I said in my book, when people go to a mountain resort, they should go as adventurers. Not having beautiful houses with all amenities. Instead, they should go and work there, trekking, camping, adventure sports. Not have spas and huge buildings to take care of all their comforts. That is what I tried to say in that book, which is what is happening in many of our hill stations, building going on, so much construction going on that the hills are getting spoilt.

Me: Due to agriculture. In Ooty, potato cultivation has caused terracing to the hillside. The whole scenery is spoilt. Man-animal conflict, too, happens, usually with elephants.

Mrs. Sinha: Really, they come into the city? In Hazaribagh area, elephants are in conflict with humans. You know, the wild elephants, not the other ones, they have come into towns and have destroyed buildings and mud huts. So people are very scared. But there must be something . . . you know, what can you do about this? They tried to kill the elephants because they don't want them to come and destroy their villages. But other solution has to be found. The government has to think of a way of preventing this. But that is happening very often. Elephants coming into the town and outlying villages.

Me: It happens in Coimbatore very often. Elephants walk into the city, especially the outlying areas.

Mrs.Sinha: Accha . . .Something is happening in Hazaribagh in Jharkhand. But you know, we had gone to Sri Lanka and I found they have a huge area just for elephants. And they have this Elephant Park or something. But elephants are just allowed to roam about, you know, in a very natural way. I feel there is in Kerala also, something.

Me: Not in a natural environment.

Mrs.Sinha: The one we saw was totally natural. It is called Elephant Park. It is like a park and animals kept there and fed there and people could come and look at them It is not as if they were just roaming around in the wild like in Kerala. So man has to think of some way of giving space and . . .

Me: Recently, I read a book about monkeys invading a school. The mother of a little child explains that they do that because their houses as well as the houses of all their relatives are destroyed.

Mrs.Sinha: What about the monkeys in Delhi? They all come to your house. Lots of monkeys! And they go to our vegetable garden and pull up all the plants. They are fond of potatoes. They really destroy everything in our garden. But what can we do? Have to have some space. We don't have any space. So people tried to bring in langurs. You know what langurs are?

Me: Yes.

Me: Yes.

Mrs.Sinha: Black-faced monkeys. Because monkeys are supposed to be scared of langurs. If a langur roams around in the garden, the monkeys don't come. But then Menaka Gandhi said that this was being cruel to the langurs . .. and she stopped it. So we were back where we were! Monkeys are still raiding our garden and one can do nothing. And the monkeys also go to the Secretarial building. You see them all over the corridors. Once, I had cone to AIMS. Somebody was sick. I was going up the stairs and I found a monkey coming down the stairs. Me: It was scary?

Mrs.Sinha: Very scary. I had to shrink myself into a corner and wait for the monkey to depart. So, you see, man-animal conflict and its prevention as well as the degradation of the natural environment are some of the areas to be explored by authors. This can be useful to the children.

Me: Thank you, Mam!

DR.IRA SAXENA

QUESTIONS TO AUTHORS OF CHILDREN'S FICTION
Q:Though environmental education is part of the curriculum of schools, fiction can play a vital role in imparting ecological values. Do you agree? If yes, please explicate.
Ans: I have firm faith in the potential of literature and the impact of stories in cultivating values from childhood and acquiring a way of life to healing stress in adult life. The love for environment glides into the thought processes of a child from the mythological stories (might of nature against demon, power of sun, lightening, *vayu, agni* , forests etc. It is only natural these tales create awareness towards the preservation of environment. In stories, for example the river appears as the giver, warmth of the sun to procreate.
Q:Many authors and illustrators (or both) are lovers or nature. Some are conservationists, wildlife photographers, etc. Please share with us some of your experiences.
Ans: As I said stories which I heard from my grandfather left an impression on me. Then my mother, a poet and writer painted colorful word pictures of aspects of nature. I noticed the beauty in

rain drops, daintiness of flowers, force of wind and of course, my heart leapt up 'when I behold the rainbow in the sky'.

In my childhood I could not explain my repulsion hearing brave-a-do adventures of my Uncle (a Forest Conservator) describing shooting tigers and going on shikar. I did not find killing of innocent beasts as something heroic. Then some pictures like denudation of trees along the Shivalik range looking like an army of mute, helpless, limbless soldiers stung in my memory shaking me up through and through.

Q:Love of nature automatically brings about understanding and awareness. Do your stories have nature as their background?
Ans: Most stories, and nature comes to aid rather than obstruct.

Q:What effect does nature have on the character of your protagonists?
Ans: I find reflections of my feelings in my characters....

Q:Do the children in your books behave in an eco-friendly manner?
Ans: Some of the characters are driven by their urges to conserve nature.

Q:What is their attitude to the conservation and pollution?
Ans: The attitude towards conservation and pollution is not shown obviously in fiction rather it becomes apparent in actions.

Q:Are they activists or passive observers?
Ans: Heroes of children's fiction cannot be passive; they prove themselves through expressive action.

Q:What is the "message' of your books regarding environmental problems, dilemmas and solutions?
Ans: *Curse of Grass*, my novel based on the beginning of Chipko movement is out and out a treatise on environmental problems. *For the Green Planet*, a science fiction deals with protection of earth. My picture book *Panna – The Lonely Duckling* presents solutions

to difficulties coming in way of clean environment. Many of my short stories deal with environmental problems e.g. The Last Call relate the conflict with poachers in a sanctuary. Whenever this young *mahaout* yelled out to his friend *rajah*, the tiger it showed itself to the tourists. In his struggle with the poachers he resolves never to call.

Q:Are animals portrayed in a realistic and healthy manner?
Ans: There is collection of pet stories *Chunnudada's Farmhouse* centering around love for animals.

Q:Comment on the relationship of your protagonists to the flora and fauna of their land.Do you adopt a positive approach to the traditional way of life, especially the lives of traditional communities?
Ans: It is necessary to tune in with the present to express meaningfulness to pre-existing beliefs. It has to be positive to ensure confidence among children.

Q:How do you work in tandem with your illustrator to project your ideas?
Ans: Whenever I get a chance I try to research along with the illustrator without overstepping on his domain. *Fascinating Folktales* is an example of my dream book developed with the confidence of the publisher and a painstaking illustrator. It was a great learning experience in folk art of India.

Q:Comment on the illustrations in your books.
Ans: I have been lucky throughout.

Q:Have you anything to say about the encouragement given by your publisher/others?
Ans: Motivation can creep in from amazing sources. Philosophies, non-violence and Gandhian thought is a constant force to guide and activate.

Q:In your opinion, is ecology and the natural environment adequately represented in fiction for children and young adults in India?
Ans: There is a vast vacuum in children's literature, many more books are required.

Q: Can more be done? Have you, personally, any plans?
Ans: Of course. Definitely I will approach this issue but currently I am in middle of an intrinsic plot of seeping hatred, not for children, for adults. A novel in Hindi, of an exemplary heroine set in the background of freedom movement of India and a novel of complex ecommerce computer software and terrorists' intrusion for young adults is in press.

Q:Please give us your opinions/suggestions
Ans: More awareness of children's books should be created. More books published and libraries set up. Teachers/librarians need to equip themselves with latest publications and the genre needs to be studied methodically in higher studies.

QUESTIONS TO YA AUTHORS

Q:The youth of today can play a crucial role in averting ecological disaster.
Yet one does not find much about the environment in ya fiction. Please comment.
Ans: Most research in environment entails use of technology. A combination of technocrat and author would be an ideal combination to write about ecological disasters and how to prevent it in fiction.

Q:As an author of young adult fiction, how have you represented nature, ecology, eco-friendly practices, etc. in your books?
Ans: Environment exists like a solid support in the background. In rural setting ecology seems to raise its head more obviously

through seemingly inane characters full of wisdom of the soil, using the natural habitat to their advantage and so on.

Q: Have you tried to bring in the love of nature in your fiction?

Ans: Always, effortlessly and deliberately.

Q: Does YA fiction pander to the dreams of westernized, urbanized youth?

Ans: YA fiction, particularly modern issues, newer dilemmas and problems of youth is fairly low in recent publications. A whole monument of literary expressions is required. The modern YA publications mirror urban society in particular.

For the western youth there are abundant choices which can be identified with by the youth of metros and urban areas. Contrastingly the rural youth is not so lucky. While they may be able to enjoy the current fiction there is shortage of books which deal with the problems of modern Ya of small towns and villages. Their problems different from those of urban youth are more intense, challenging and very often life threatening. On one hand they are close to nature they are least considered for providing solutions to ecological difficulties.

Q: What can authors do to remind youth of their responsibilities regarding the environment?

Ans: All authors need to do is remind themselves of human contribution to nature since their attitudes will slide in automatically in their work.

Q: Many authors and illustratiors (or both) are lovers or nature. Some are conservationists, wildlife photographers, etc. Please share with us some of your experiences.

Ans: I have done this.

SHAMIM PADAMSEE

Shamim Padamsee is keenly interested in early childhood learning and is director of an educational organisation that runs schools in Maharashtra, Gujarat and Andhra Pradesh. She lives in Mumbai and in her spare time, dreams up stories like *Dancing on Walls*, her first book for children, and *Birdywood Buzz: The Vulture Returns*, both published by Tulika. Her website, youngindiabooks.com., showcases books for children published in India.

Though environmental education is part of the curriculum of schools, fiction can play a vital role in imparting ecological values. Do you agree? If yes, please explicate.

Yes, fiction does play a very important part. It reinforces the learning from school because stories help children connect with the flora, fauna and nature on apersonal level. Once children are drawn to a character , albeit an anthropomorphic one, they feel a deep connect and hence wou;d want to protect and nurture them.

Many authors and illustrators (or both) are lovers or nature. Some are conservationists, wildlife photographers, etc. Please share with us some of your experiences.

I am a nature buff and am happiest when out in the wild – mountains, jungles. Most of my stories have been inspired when I am in connect with nature. Example – *Birdywood Buzz*.

Love of nature automatically brings about understanding and awareness. Do your stories have nature as their background?
Many of them do.

Are they activists or passive observers?
They are activists. In *The Magic Jharoka* aseries, the protagonistsactuallyhelp in capturingpoachers.

Are animals portrayed in a realistic and healthy manner?
Yes

SHOBHA THAROOR SRINIVASAN

Shobha Tharoor Srinivasan is a California-based non-profit development consultant, a non-profit grant writer working for

individuals with disabilities for almost two decades, professional voice talent, model, poet, translator and children's author. Her voice has been used in documentaries, educational and journalistic initiatives, and audio books, and her essays and stories have appeared in publications including 'India Currents' and 'Skipping Stones'. Her poem, "Animal Groups," was published in a 2014 Her books include 'A Pie Surprise and Other Stories' (Mango, 2011) and 'Around the World You Wander' (Schlostic, 2010). She also happens to be the sister of the distinguished Sashi Tharoor.

QUESTIONS TO AUTHORS OF CHILDREN'S FICTION
Though environmental education is part of the curriculum of schools, fiction can play a vital role in imparting ecological values. Do you agree? If yes, please explicate.
Absolutely. Fiction can bring issues alive in colourful ways. A well written story can spark interest in ecological issues that may otherwise remain in a school book. Stories can stimulate the emotion of readers, help them learn, and encourage them to respond to the environment in new ways.

Many authors and illustrators (or both) are lovers or nature. Some are conservationists, wildlife photographers, etc. Please share with us some of your experiences.
For some people travel is a way to see the world, but books can be another way to experience new places, ideas and things. I am a "traveler" like Tennyson's Ulysses always looking toward the next vista: "all experience is an arch wherethro' Gleams that untravell'd world whose margin fades For ever and forever when I move." As the inimitable Dr. Suess says "oh the places you will go" in the world of books and stories.

Love of nature automatically brings about understanding and awareness. Do your stories have nature as their background?
I have translated an ecologically themed Hindi book called (in English) "An Autobiography of a Tree". In addition I have a yet unpublished story called "Sandalwood's Advice" that celebrates the differences in Nature and our shared relationship with the earth. As a Voice Over Artist I have been the Narrator for a number of ecologically themed films.

What effect does nature have on the character of your protagonists?
Nature usually teaches us that we are all part of a shared world. While celebrating our differences, Nature shows the universal in all of us.

Do the children in your books behave in an eco-friendly manner?
I hope they do. My protagonists, as evidenced in the published works so far, are all mindful of others and caring and giving.

What is their attitude to conservation and pollution?
Not sure that my stories have addressed conservation and pollution specifically. But, as a Voice artist I have been a narrator recently in a film about plastic pollution in pilgrimage sites in Kerala.

Are they activists or passive observers?
They are proactive and participatory. They question and they engage.

What is the "message' of your books regarding environmental problems, dilemmas and solutions?
I have been a "story teller" and communicator all my life. As a non-profit grant writer working for individuals with disabilities for almost two decades, I used the "power" of words and the stories of people to draw funders to programs that they wished to support. My first published book sprung from my tenure in philanthropy-all three protagonists in <u>A Pie Surprise and Other Stories</u> published by Mango Books, came up with creative plans to "give" to another. These stories were later selected for a literary reader as a skill based interactive series for 5th graders in India.

Are animals portrayed in a realistic and healthy manner?
No animals in my stories other than the animal protagonists in my retelling of Native American Folktales.

Comment on the relationship of your protagonists to the flora and fauna of their land.
Nature is respected and valued in the stories and the mythology of Native Americans

Do you adopt a positive approach to the traditional way of life, especially the lives of traditional communities?
I celebrate tradition and value history as a way for us to learn of what came before and what lies ahead.

How do you work in tandem with your illustrator to project your ideas?
N/A The selection of an illustrator usually lies with the publisher

Comment on the illustrations in your books.
They have complemented my stories admirably.

Have you anything to say about the encouragement given by your publisher/others? Can authors dispel misconceptions, for example prejudices against animals eg. "blind as a bat"?
They can and they should.

In your opinion, is ecology and the natural environment adequately represented in fiction for children and young adults in India?
N/A I live abroad and am not as familiar with fiction for young adults in India as I should be.

Can more be done? Have you, personally, any plans?

All my creative efforts, as a writer and Voice Artist are to draw young minds toward and understanding an appreciation of the beauty and wonder of our Natural world. I have worked as a Narrator for many environment themed short films and will continue to be available for socially conscious projects.

BENITA SEN

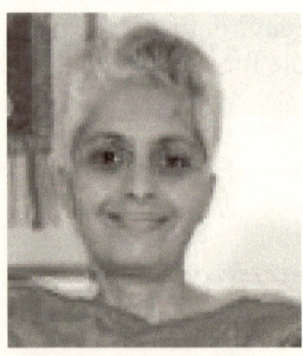

Journalist and children's author, Benita Sen has written dozens of books -- fiction and non-fiction -- for children and young people. These have been published by Children's Book Trust, Pratham, Rupa & Co, Scholastic and Teri Press among others. She was the long-time and extremely popular editor of Target, which published many short stories of ecological interest. A crafts book on reusing waste material has been published by Scholastic. She volunteers with several not-for-profit organizations in the health and environment sectors. She is a resource person teaching environmental issues, and telling children stories.

QUESTIONS TO AUTHORS OF CHILDREN'S FICTION
Q: Though environmental education is part of the curriculum of schools, fiction can play a vital role in imparting ecological values. Do you agree? If yes, please explicate.
A: Absolutely. Reinforcement is an integral part of the learning process, so repeating the same message in different places (in this instance, different subject spaces) can only support the importance of the message. Also, sadly, even today, environmental education is not perceived by many students as important as, say, Mathematics. Therefore, the message in the content carries less punch than it ought to. So, repeating the message wherever relevant can help drive it home faster and further.

Q: Many authors and illustratiors (or both) are lovers or nature. Some are conservationists, wildlife photographers, etc. Please share with us some of your experiences.
A: I believe in voluntarism and work with raising trees, planting hedges and trees and with animal adoptions.

I grew up in a tiny home that had less space for us and more for plants and animals. Injured, lonely, scared and ill cats and birds knew they could find succor in this home and even today, my mother, aged 87 years, shares food and space with sparrows and bulbuls and cats. So it was natural for me to grow up loving fellow creatures (how do humans forget that they are also animals?!). I adore Indian neighbourhood dogs and my worried father even asked a doctor if I could be given prophylactic anti-rabies shots. In those days, there were none. I still rescue and rehabilitate abandoned pets or neighbourhood dogs in distress or lost puppies.

I married into the Army, an organization that cherishes greenery and life. We live amidst Nature and what comes with it. For instance, our current house is old and teems with millipedes. Rather than kill them when they enter the room, we place them outdoors. Our last house had at least 26 lizards but they were never shooed away nor killed since it was more their house than ours. Yes, I did get an occasional scare when they fell on me, but apart from a startled scream from me, we lived in harmony. I have lived on the outskirts of a forest and a wildlife sanctuary with chital feeding off the hedge, nilgai bolting across the road and wild boar crashing into hedgerows. For the last 28 years, I have grown trees from seeds of fruit that I eat or collected seedlings from under mother trees, nurtured them and planted them around me or distributed them. That makes for hundreds of hedges and trees.

As a voluntarist, I have worked/am working as a volunteer for several NGOs including Atree (as an environmental educator), and as an editor with organizations like Nature Forever Society (Save the Sparrows) and Make A Wish Foundation of India.

Our home has always been a sanctuary for birds and we have encouraged nesting birds although nests can be messy and inconvenient (if they nest outside your window, you cannot open it till the babies have flown!). Even in my current workplace, I plant hedges and climbers because those are major nesting sites. We put up nest boxes wherever we go since our favourite bird, the House Sparrow, is fighting a losing battle. It is a cavity nester and needs us to provide food and safe nesting places. We are currently fostering an Indian neighbourhood dog that met with an accident and lost a leg.

Q: Love of nature automatically brings about understanding and awareness. Do your stories have nature as their background?
A: Since my life is incomplete without plants and animals, virtually all my stories weave themselves around the natural world in some way. Most of my work involves nature. My book, *Oly and Owly* is about a little girl and an owlet and how they finally meet. Another book, *A Whale of a Time* deals with a little boy and a young whale and how they learn to respect each other's strengths and limitations and still be friends. Both have won prizes from CBT and been published.

I write both fact and fiction books and my report, *May You Find a Mountain To Climb* has won an award from CBT. That's where publishers come into play: they need to encourage more such books.

Q: What effect does nature have on the character of your protagonists?
A: My protagonists are comfortable with other creatures and with greenery. In BIRD OF PEACE, written on invitation for AWIC's collection, The Road to Peace, the protagonist, Pramiti advises friends before a 'peace' meet in school: "Don't go around chopping trees down. No damaging branches." Then, when there's talk of releasing doves, she says, "Why hold a peace meet if you can't be at peace with Nature?"

In my latest book *What Did Nepo Do With A Sari*? (published by Katha), the child and the grandparents live in peaceful co-existence with the dog and the cat and even the mouse, Nengti. When the grandparents and the child go out to solve the mystery, so do the dog, the cat and the mouse. They're just as curious and as much a part of the family procession!

Q: Do the children in your books behave in an eco-friendly manner?
A: Oh yes! They're responsible citizens, even if they are young. And it is the responsibility of each of us to show concern for other forms of life. Since I have been an environmental educator, wherever I can, I bring in finer nuances like, don't pluck a blade of grass unless you have to. Even my fiction is researched and apart from a little poetic license, I offer my reader facts.

Q: What is their attitude to the conservation and pollution?
A: I write more for very young readers. They are aware of the issues.

Q: Are they activists or passive observers?
A: They will not do something anti-environmental, deliberately. That's positive reinforcement. Some, like in *Bird of Peace*, are activists. In fact, *Yakity Yak*, (my book for very young readers which was selected by an independent body of authors for the 5th Nami Island International Children's Book Festival in Korea and listed for Vodafone Crossword Book Award 2009 for Children) is about a talkative young yak who is friends with the grass and apologises to it before eating it, friendly with flowers and clouds and the wind.

Q: What is the "message' of your books regarding environmental problems, dilemmas and solutions?
A: Be thoughtful, be considerate, reduce your carbon footprint, do away with practices that don't make sense or harm other forms of life simply for a ceremony.

Q: Comment on the relationship of your protagonists to the flora and fauna of their land.
A: They are almost never in conflict even if there is a little discomfort. Even in *Cottonopolis*, published by Rupa & Co in a collection called *A Leaf Out of My Book*, the tree has the last laugh over grandfather.

Q: Do you adopt a positive approach to the traditional way of life, especially the lives of traditional communities?
A: Yes. Two of my books (*It's Fair to Share* and *First Farmers*) are Warli stories that celebrate the simplicity and the respect Warlis have for the land and its produce. These two books have

been selected by the Kendriya Vidyalaya Sangathan as recommended reading for its libraries across India.

Q: How do you work in tandem with your illustrator to project your ideas?

A: Some publishers do not encourage much interaction but for my latest book, *What Did Nepo Do With A Sari*? I selected the illustrator, Sekhar Mukherjee, and interacted extensively with him on my vision.

Q: Comment on the illustrations in your books.

A: Since I write a lot for the very young reader, most of my books are heavily illustrated. I wish the stories for older children would also have more illustrations.

Q: Have you anything to say about the encouragement given by your publisher/others?

A: A writer's world is a lonesome cocoon but I must acknowledge author Paro Anand who encouraged me to send in my poems (I write in prose and verse, fiction and fact books) and stories when she was commissioning for Rupa & Co. My editor at Teri, Pallavi Sah, understood and appreciated my bent of mind and we began several eco-friendly projects together. One, which has not yet been published, is a fact and fiction series that touches on creatures around us. Scholastic has encouraged me to do books on recycled crafts, of which one has been published, and one is in the pipeline.

,*Q: Can authors dispel misconceptions, for example prejudices against animals eg."blind as a bat"?*

A: Absolutely! I do so wherever I can. Even my fiction is researched. For instance, in one story, I pointed out that bird-brained is not a very apt description for someone with lower intelligence since birds are highly intelligent. In a song (Titli Urhti Chali Doooor Chhorkey Dhool) I wrote for the TV show *Galli Galli Sim Sim,* I observed the flight of butterflies as the dust rose in gusts, before writing it.

We all celebrate the dance of a peacock but have you ever thought of how awkward it can get to move around with so many feathers, especially when they are wet? *Wish That Went Whoosh* (Rupa & Co) is a poem-story about that. This observation is courtesy the fact that there were peacocks living in our compound and so, as neighbours, you observe them for hours!

Q: In your opinion, is ecology and the natural environment adequately represented in fiction for children and young adults in India?

A: There is scope to do much more, both in the genres of fact and fiction books. I have worked and lived closely with Nature all my life and I believe not only should we write more about such issues but also take children out through book promotions or author interactions to be in touch with the environment around them.

My daughter Moen Sen, a PhD scholar and I have written a series of books on renewable sources of energy for Teri. LINK: http://bookstore.teriin.org/searchresult.php

Publishers need to encourage green ideas. I am grateful to Teri for their series, Smart Green Civilisations LINK http://bookstore.teriin.org/child_book_inside.php?material_id=630 which brought out how comfortable our ancestors were living a low-carbon footprint life.

Q: Can more be done? Have you, personally, any plans? Please give us your opinions/suggestions

A: Of course! The environment is taking a beating every breath we take. We need to look at the issue from various aspects. This includes consulting energy and ecology experts on 'green' offices for publishers, more e-books, using recycled paper, apart from encouraging authors who write on environment-friendly issues. I have travelled extensively through rural India and I wonder how many urban children realize that the thatched huts they draw to depict a village in art class, are rarely seen in, say, states like Punjab. You have to go right up to the border near Khasa before you can see thatched huts. So, I look forward to encouragement from our schools, teachers, publishers, editors, bookstores to write about this contemporary India.

I want to do a book of environment-friendly plays for very young readers, but have found no taker so far. Anyone out there interested?

QUESTIONS TO YA AUTHORS

Q: The youth of today can play a crucial role in averting ecological disaster. Yet one does not find much about the environment in ya fiction. Please comment.
A: Good question! Is it the chicken-and-egg situation? There IS demand but perhaps... just perhaps, since I have not officially studied the phenomenon, publishers need to push more and more environmentalists need to come forward and write. You see, these ARE special areas. Unless you have (a) interest (b) some knowledge (c) first-hand experience, it is difficult to write a convincing, interersting piece. I am grateful to CBT that my report, *May You Find a Mountain To Climb*, has won a prize. It is about Wing Commander Prafulla Rao, who lives in Kalimpong and is trying to raise awareness and action to save the sliding hills. I wanted to do a book for YA with five or six such environmental crusaders but found no takers.

QAs an author of young adult fiction, how have you represented nature, ecology, eco-friendly practices, etc. in your books?
A: The same as above. I research my facts and then try to make them interesting. For instance, we believe Fall comes once a year, before winter. Anyone who has lived in the hills would know better. Around March, there are many, many trees that shed their leaves.

Q: If your protagonists are involved with nature, are they passive observers or activists.
A: Both. Activism is a strong word and a major commitment, so they also need to get their facts and priorities and values right at that age, before launching off on activism. Perhaps I'd say, they strive for a greener world.

Q: Have you tried to bring in the love of nature in your fiction?
A: I don't really try to do that but it comes out since I am so fond of the natural world. Even a tree, in *Bouncer Ball*, a story for young readers, has a living presence. It is wary when the ball bounces too high because it is awkward about its balding crown becoming visible!

Q

Please give your suggestions/comments.
The entire system needs to gear up for a greener world: parents, schools (through Nature and Reading Clubs, perhaps), publishers, illustrators, authors, readers, teachers…

DEEPAK DALAL

Author of the popular *Vikram-Aditya* series, Deepak Dalal is a Chemical Engineer from Washington State University and holds a Bachelor's Degree in Science – Technology, Chemistry and Physics. He has taken to researching and writing of children's novel full-time and spends considerable time visiting schools for talks on books, environmental matters, conversation and creative writing. His stories typically have a strong natural history base. The idea is to create a connection between children and wildlife. For a year Deepak taught in an international school (School of the Nations) in Macau, China. Based on his Andaman novels, he was selected to attend the Highlights Children's Writers' Conference 2003 in United States. He was honoured by Sanctuary Magazine in 2004 for increasing awareness of Indian children about wildlife and ecological issues and for fostering in them a love for wild places. His two Sahyadri Adventure books were shortlisted for the Vodafone Crossword Book Award for the best children's book of the year 2011. Deepak is currently working on two children's books – A Dolphin Adventure Story set in the Arabian Sea and an illustrated series of books – the 'Feather Tales' series for younger children.

QUESTIONS TO AUTHORS OF CHILDREN'S FICTION

Though environmental education is part of the curriculum of schools, fiction can play a vital role in imparting ecological values. Do you agree? If yes, please explicate.
Fiction is the best way of conveying environmental awareness. Stories dig deep into the reader and their message (if given subtly) remains for years to come. The key here is subtle messages. Moralistic material doesn't work. A good story, delivered with good pace and plot works very well.

Though environmental education is part of the curriculum of schools, fiction can play a vital role in imparting ecological values. Do you agree? If yes, please explicate.
Fiction is the best way of conveying environmental awareness. Stories dig deep into the reader and their message (if given subtly) remains for years to come. The key here is subtle messages. Moralistic material doesn't work. A good story, delivered with good pace and plot works very well.

Many authors and illustratiors (or both) are lovers or nature. Some are conservationists, wildlife photographers, etc. Please share with us some of your experiences.
If you want to write about nature you have to love it. There is no substitute for this. The writing comes out false if you aren't the sort who loves the outdoors and yearns to spend his time in wilderness areas..

Love of nature automatically brings about understanding and awareness. Do your stories have nature as their background?
All my stories have nature, wildlife and conservation woven into them.

What effect does nature have on the character of your protagonists?
Their lives are continuously influenced by what they see and experience in wild places.

Do the children in your books behave in an eco-friendly manner?
Mostly.

What is their attitude to the conservation and pollution?
Disgust and sadness.

Are they activists or passive observers?
Active.

What is the "message' of your books regarding environmental problems, dilemmas and solutions?
Love your wilderness areas. Appreciate them and build a lasting connect with them.
Are animals portrayed in a realistic and healthy manner?
Always realistic.
Comment on the relationship of your protagonists to the flora and fauna of their land.
Visceral.
Do you adopt a positive approach to the traditional way of life, especially the lives of traditional communities?
Absolutely.
How do you work in tandem with your illustrator to project your ideas?
A good relationship is very important. Poor output if you are not in tune with the illustrator.
Comment on the illustrations in your books.
My best illustrator was a 14 year old girl with outstanding talent. She illustrated my Sahyadri books. All good illustrators have a strong ego and pride in their work.
Have you anything to say about the encouragement given by your publisher/others?
Not really.
Can authors dispel misconceptions, for example prejudices against animals eg. "blind as a bat"?
Not easy, but we try.
In your opinion, is ecology and the natural environment adequately represented in fiction for children and young adults in India?
Not at all. Real dearth of good work.
Can more be done? Have you, personally, any plans?
Always work in progress.
Please give us your opinions/suggestions
Need many, many more writers.

QUESTIONS TO YA AUTHORS
The youth of today can play a crucial role in averting ecological disaster.

Unlikely today, but certainly when they grow up. That's why write. To shape their minds for the future, that they will protect their wilderness areas when their generation is at the helm of affairs.
Yet one does not find much about the environment in ya fiction. Please comment.
So sad. Wish their were more.
Have you tried to bring in the love of nature in your fiction?
Always.
Does ya fiction pander to the dreams of westernized, urbanized youth?
This is correct to some extent but not entirely true. All children who enjoy reading read my work.
What can authors do to remind youth of their responsibilities regarding the environment?
We have to work hard at it through good stories and subtle messages.

ZAI WHITAKER

Zai Whitaker, Director of the Madras Crocodile Farm and Centre for Herpetology, has written a dozen books, most of them for children and young readers. She writes about wildlife and conservation. Her interest in this area started when she was a young girl in Mumbai, because of the several naturalists in her family. These included Dr Salim Ali the ornithologist, who is known as the Bird Man of India. After college, Zai worked at the Snake Park and Crocodile Bank in Chennai. She helped establish these trusts along with her husband, Romulus Whitaker, the Snakeman of India. At both places, she spoke and wrote about the fascinating lives of these animals, and the importance of protecting them. She has studied and worked with people of the Irula community, who are snake catchers. Zai is a director of the Irula Tribal Women's Welfare Society, which helps the community in many ways. Zai enjoys writing both fiction and non-fiction, and also poetry. Her story "What Happened to the Reptiles", with its message of communal harmony, is being used by several human rights groups to discuss this important issue with youngsters.

Though environmental education is part of the curriculum of schools, fiction can play a vital role in imparting ecological values. Do you agree? If yes, please explicate.

I think that when you look at textbooks and the kinds of facts that we give children, it has in a way very limited value. I think that fiction is a much more powerful way of getting message across to young people. And you know, from what I've seen it's through fiction children will really absorb and internalise and discuss, not by a list of dry facts in their text books.

Many authors and illustrators (or both) are lovers or nature. Some are conservationists, wildlife photographers, etc. Please share with us some of your experiences.

Yeah, I have been to a lot of forests. I have been very lucky in that sense, because my father was a conservationist, is a conservationist because he is still alive. So was my uncle, so was my ex-husband and I'm also very lucky that my present husband is very interested in wild life and conservation. I have travelled extensively in India and Indian forests. And now because of my husband is from South Africa, I also have been lucky to visit a lot of the South African National Parks for instance, Huka National Park. So it was a lovely to transition from elephant and tiger to cheetah , giraffe and zebra, that's very very exciting.

Love of nature automatically brings about understanding and awareness. Do your stories have nature as their background?

Yes, I think practically everything I have written is against the tapestry of natural history and environment and conservation. Whether it's my poems or short stories or novels or my prose, it's really all about this area.

Do the children in your books behave in an eco-friendly manner?

Yeah, they better behave in an eco-friendly manner. Yes, well one of my books *Andamans Boy*, for instance, is about a boy who doesn't start out as a passionate eco-friendly preacher. But it ends up in the Andaman Islands and finally the choice he makes at the end of the novel is to stay on in the Andamans with the Jarawa tribe rather than come back to Mumbai where a huge family legacy and lots of money is waiting for him.

So, in fact when this book was being illustrated and the publisher was giving the illustrator the book chapter by chapter and he was doing the drawings and after the last chapter, he phoned the publisher and said, "OK, now send me the next chapter." They said, "No, that's the end of the book." He said, "My god, doesn't he come back to Bombay?" And he was so horrified that he made this choice. So, yes he was a boy who made this transition from city life to the natural world. While others like Kali were actually born in an eco-friendly environment because he is part of the Irula tribe which are snake catchers.

You think this book is partly autobiographical?
I have been to the Andamans, and not autobiographical in that sense because I am not a little boy. But... I think it has a lot to do with my feelings for the islands and my interest in the development of good conservation practices in the island which unfortunately still have a long way to go.

What is the "message' of your books regarding environmental problems, dilemmas and solutions?
I think that the message is... as every book about environment, every article... that you know, time is running out, the waters are rising and we better do something quickly and it means each of us has to be more sensitive towards the environment and use it more carefully.

Are animals portrayed in a realistic and healthy manner?
Sometimes they are realistic, sometimes they start talking and so on. Especially in my book of poems which is called 'The Boastful Centipede', some of the animals do talk and kind of give a message. It's something that I thought I wouldn't do, but I did. And I really enjoyed it.

Which author or novelist influenced you the most, because you may have some model, any one when you were young some writer must have affected you, if at all, any writer?
I think, you know, I started out with... I know that Robin Hood was one of my favourite stories. Maybe it was because so much of it happened in Sherwood Forest, I don't know. And then later Enid Blyton...Famous Five and all those books and then I think very earlier on, I started reading Louisa May Alcott, Jane Austen. And Jane Austen remains one of my favourite authors, one of the authors who you know, over a long stretch has remained my

favourite author. In terms of wildlife, Jim Corbett and Ruskin Bond, probably. Gavin Maxwell who wrote about the otters.

Comment on the illustrations in your books. Are you happy with the way in which your books have been illustrated

Yes, I am. In every book, there is something that you think could have been better. But on the whole I'm really very happy and I have worked with a wide range of illustrators. And I was very lucky because, in fact, apart from my book of poems, the other books were just given to the illustrators by the publishers. It wasn't that I was sitting with them and explaining to them the themes. So, I did talk to them. I did respond to the earlier illustrations and made some comments. But on the whole, they worked independently and I think with each of my books, they have really got the spirit of the book just as I would have wanted them to. So, I have been lucky and very satisfied.

Especially with Aadivaasi children, it's a very sensitive thing, you don't want them to look... you want them to look appropriate... slightly different but not outlandish. So, I think the illustrators have done a good job.

To which state do the Aadivasi children of your book belong ?

Aadivaasi Children of Tamilnadu. Well, Kali is from Tamilnadu and actually is now a young man with two children of his own. But he used to be my son's playmate and they used to go off catching frogs, scorpions and water snakes when they were children. So when I wrote this book, I spoke to him before and I said, "Look, I am planning to write a story using your name. He said, " O yes, you must bring the book and show it to me." So, I did and he liked the illustrations. It has also been ranslated into Tamil and so I gave him a copy of that.

Have you anything to say about the encouragement given by your publisher/others?

Yes, I have had a lot of encouragement from publishers and you know, the trend is that the authors should be angry with the publishers. But I'm not except that of course nobody earns a paisa out of writing. But that's another story. But...

My publishers have been very supportive and very encouraging and very often really pushed me like in *Andamans Boy* which was written because two of the editors from the publishing company came to see me and said, "Please write a novel for young children." And I said, "Don't be silly. How can you write a novel for young children? It should be short stories." And we had a big argument and they said, "No. You should do it." So, I did. And I would never have done it if they had not pushed me and supported me. So I think I am lucky with my publishers.

Please give us your opinions/suggestions

I just would like to make one more comment about children's writing. I feel that you know, publishers are… what seems to happen a lot is that publishers are very enthusiastic at the beginning and then after the book is published, of course there are exceptions… and I think Tulika is an exception… but sometimes after the book is finished, there is not enough of an effort to distribute the book and I think that would be a make a huge difference. For example, I have just written a book about the Andamans for children called *Magic Islands*, which is about the history and the natural history of the Andamans. It is about the whole Aadhivaasi history which is just so sad and such an important lesson for our government and for us as civilians of India. And you know the mistakes we made in terms of the environment…what we need to do better… I did a lot of research and met a lot of naturalists. I went back to the Andamans and I interviewed people…

And now the book is out but I don't see any great efforts to distribute it. And that's really disappointing because it was written with a focus and as I said, time is running out specially for fragile island ecosystems like the Andamans and so you would really want publishers to put more of an effort and push in the book .After all a lot of my time and energy has gone into it from their side as well as the writers' side. So, you know, use it as a resource.

[May be the government should take steps. And this is the government's The National Book Trust.]

Can authors dispel misconceptions, for example prejudices against animals eg. "blind as a bat"?

Well I think, they are not blind, they depend on their sonar more than the eyesight. So to some extent it's true. And also I think it's fine for language to take liberties like this. But, what I have tried to do in my poems for instance is ... unfortunately don't have that book here, but I read a lot about the animal and tried to make it as true to science as possible. I think that is also important as a writer.

Do you think more books should come out for children?
Yeah, the more the better. But it is very, very important ...not just books coming out as I said, books being used, books being distributed .Children being involved in the production of books...some lovely literature has come out which has started with a dialogue with children.

And I find as a teacher for example that I am always asking my students, "Do you like this? Do you like that? Why did you like this story?" .And it gives you amazing feedback because children are so straightforward and honest, unlike adults. And so I think it's a huge resource, what we should use.

As an educated women, a teacher, what is your contribution?
Well, I am teacher and I have been teaching for eighteen years.. and quite often when my children...my students have done assignments, for example when we have a creative writing unit or a journaling unit...then I will also write something at that time. The students are share what they have written, I also read what I have written, and their responses are very, very valuable, very useful and very honest. They will say, "O Miss !we don't like that as much as what you have wrote before...and so it's a huge resource and it also makes the classes much more equal...you are doing the same work as the students. They have the opportunity to respond to what you have written.

And I feel it's very important and a huge drawback of our education in India is that it's so undemocratic and we teachers standing on a platform and the students are shivering with fright. This makes the whole thing much more equal and democratic.

How do you find the time to write all these books?
I try to write something, a little bit every day, even it's for fifteen minutes. And sometimes I just write a little haiku.Haikus are great because they are so short .But I think practically everything I have written, and I have written 13 books... most of them while I was

teaching...so you know, the big bonus about being a teacher is the holidays, you get the summer holidays and then the winter break and so that's my time to write. Quite often, I have started something during the holidays and then finished it during term, using weekends and the nights. *Andamans Boy* was written when I was on sabbatical. The school very kindly allowed me to go away for a year and do some writing for the school and as well as whatever I wanted....that's when *Andamans Boy* was written.

Do they prescribe this in some of the schools in India?

Yes they do. I think, *Kaali* as well but the most prescribed book is a short story called "What happened to the Reptiles?" And that's after Ayodhya. A group of writers in Delhi got together and decided to do something for students [children] in terms of discrimination and pluralism and so on. So they put together a collection of short stories called *Saahi, Best Friend* and asked me to write a story and so I wrote a story called "What happened to the Reptiles?" which is basically about how these animals are living happily in a forest.

And then they decide that the snakes are bad and say, "Let's kick them out." And then of course the rat population increases. .And then they say, "The turtles are so funny- looking - they have the shells and they are so slow. So, we don't want turtles in our community." So then all the fruits that fell to the forest floor were rotting and the place became so stinky. And so, of course the message being you need everyone to make a wholesome community.

The story has been picked up by about I think six or eight different ICSE, SSLC and Matric text books and translated into several languages and that's very satisfying because it was written for that purpose. The children are actually reading and benefitting from it.

And it's been made into plays. In fact a few years ago, I saw a wonderful group of a special school for disabled handicapped children... they performed it. The main character who is a crocodile was a blind boy. He just performed it so beautifully and that was really very heartening to see...

Your ex-husband is a specialist in King Cobra...have you written anything about King Cobra?

Yeah. But an interesting fact is that…they are fascinating snakes and they are endangered now, because for any big animal, like say… I suppose the mammal counterpart, would be the elephant … habitat is dwindling, the forest shrinking, being encroached and used for human purposes. So the king Cobra's habitat is really dwindling and of course you have this big poisonous snake, people want to kill it. But there are still pockets like Agumbe in Karnataka and places in the Andaman Islands, where they are still surviving.

Due to the climate change, the snakes are slowly coming up to hills!

Yeah, You know an interesting thing is happening…you are right. Rat snakes never used to be here. But just at school the other day, a colleague of mine said, "O, I saw a big snake in my garden." When she described it, it was obvious that it was a rat snake which you would never see up here, even you know eight -ten years ago. But the other thing that is happening is that there are some snakes that used to be very common up here like the Euro-pelted which are sheild tailed snakes, with blunt tails which are burrowers. When I first came to Kodai in the 80s, you would be walking along, you know, and a gardener would be digging …they will be digging by the roadside… and they would say, "we just saw a snake" and they would pull out a dead snake they had just killed or in the garden if you were digging, you would see them… but now you don't see them. And this is you know , because of the dryness and the heat…

Like the sparrows which are in danger of becoming extinct.?

I am happy to say we have some sparrows in our house.

Well, thank you for sparing your valuable time for us.

It's a pleasure,

RANJIT LAL

Ranjit Lal is a freelance writer cum columnist for over two decades. He has written over 1,000 articles, short stories, features and photo-features that have been published in over 50 newspapers and magazines. He writes on natural history (birds and birding), photography (birds and nature), humour, satire and automobiles. He also writes for children and young adults.

Ranjit wrote: "Hi, Have you seen my book, 'Wild City' published (but now out of print!) by Penguin? The intro there should cover the bonding with nature part! My take re writing on the subject for kids is simple: I had a ball roaming around whether it was in a large garden, beach or sanctuary when I was a kid; you could let your imagination go wacko; later of course, the questions arose: Why, why not, how, when, where? etc. How the hell did a bird the size of a sparrow fly all the way from Siberia to winter in your 20X20 ft garden - and keep coming year after year? And hundreds more such...(which, I'm still asking!). The stories followed and drawing analogies was the simplest way to do that (as in 'The Caterpillar Who Went on a Diet' and 'When Banshee Kissed Bimbo.' And of course, the crows in Crow Chronicles and the monkeys in The Life and Times of Altu Faltu.) You observe, make the connection and your story virtually writes itself! Kids these days are separated too much from 'nature' - if not afraid of even the creatures that can be found in homes and gardens (geckos, cockroaches, mice, rats...etc.). Having said that, it seems many of them (or their parents) did enjoy the creepy crawlies in Caterpillar! Feedback is sparse but usually encouraging (though again sometimes you wonder how much this is because usually teachers/parents are looking on, to make sure nothing is said that might hurt the great author's 'sentiments'!!) I don't know about children's books in general and their connections with 'nature'; all I do know is that I enjoy writing about birds, bees (!) beasts etc. and hope kids enjoy reading about them. I've 'moved on' to writing about humans now, too, but every now and then revert back to the animal kingdom... Cheers, Ranjit"

LEELA GOUR BROOME

Leela Gour Broome is a teacher and committed environmentalist. She has degrees in Western classical music and English Literature. For two decades she has combined music and literature with her love for nature by directing nature and environment camps for kids on her farm with her husband. She has years of experience teaching music and performing arts to children, and has conducted workshops for teachers in music, the performing arts, and creative writing. She also conducts book-reading sessions, language- and literature-related workshops for schools and at literature festivals around the country. Her short stories and cartoons have been published in several publications. Among her books are:: *Flute in the Forest, Red Kite Adventure, The Anaishola Chronicle* and *The Earthquake Boy.*

QUESTIONS TO AUTHORS OF CHILDREN'S FICTION

Though environmental education is part of the curriculum of schools, fiction can play a vital role in imparting ecological values. Do you agree? If yes, please explicate.

A: I agree. Indian school children have to swallow EE (Environment Education) from the junior classes onwards, in varying degrees from year to year. Most of this is quite negative in scenario portrayed by their text books and teachers. They also get plenty of this on TV and in their daily newspapers, even in their daily practical lives. So, what they do study /test /see, is unfortunately quite negative. Fiction can play the positive role, in that protagonists of our fiction could be doing positive actions, from which positive outcomes will take place. I feel children of all ages need positive material to imbibe good habits and carry out good actions, rather than learn about all the negative.

Many authors and illustrators (or both) are lovers of nature. Some are conservationists, wildlife photographers, etc. Please share with us some of your experiences.

A: I have loved nature from my childhood, and I was lucky to live in several outlying areas of the cities of yesteryear! Fishing, camping in the wild, travelling by car through much of central and north India provided me with valuable geography/history/cultural lessons here. My first ten years after marriage were spent on the beautiful wild hills and valleys of South Indian tea plantations, where I came in contact with wilderness, learnt about conservation, and realized how very valuable our wild forests and lands were.

When my husband and I moved to our farm outside Pune, ten years later, we launched Nature Trails Camps for kids between ages 7 and 12 years, and introduced them to Indian flora, and fauna through EE camps, nature study, farming, forestry, birdlife, mountain climbing, outdoor adventure – the intention being that if they understood how valuable our wild spaces were, well, they would grow to value it and from that would follow the care for this. This we did for 16 hectic years. When it became too tiring for us, we closed camps, and I finally took to writing fiction for the same age group, and with environment (this time both wilderness and urban) as my main focus.

Love of nature automatically brings about understanding and awareness. Do your stories have nature as their background?

A: Yes they do, but as most of my readers are urban dwellers, I've incorporated nature in the city as well. Comments about litter/garbage/social and civic sense are made when relevant.

What effect does nature have on the character of your protagonists?
A: In two of my books, nature has a major effect on my protagonists. I use my main characters to promote nature and animal well-being, through their comments or thinking, or through general conversations with other characters.

Do the children in your books behave in an eco-friendly manner?
A: Yes. Always.

What is their attitude to the conservation and pollution?
A: As my characters in these two books are based in forest or wilderness areas, they understand and appreciate conservation.

Are they activists or passive observers?
A: They are passive observers, but follow forest rules, valuing them.

What is the "message' of your books regarding environmental problems, dilemmas and solutions? What effect does nature have on the character of your protagonists?
A: As my characters are comfortable in nature, and appreciate their surroundings, their comments and thoughts usually promote these simple messages. No environmental problems were discussed, other than expected general and tourist codes of behavior with wild animals in such areas.

Are animals portrayed in a realistic and healthy manner?
A: Always, unless human interference has led to animal aggression. I will then explain why this was so.

Comment on the relationship of your protagonists to the flora and fauna of their land.
A: Pride and valued the flora and fauna around them.

Do you adopt a positive approach to the traditional way of life, especially the lives of traditional communities?
A: Yes. This is evident in *Flute in the Forest*, where Kurumbas and their way of life was described in a nutshell.

How do you work in tandem with your illustrator to project your ideas?
A: My publishers, so far, have chosen their own illustrators. I was invited to give my comments about the Book Cover, and my suggestions on one were accepted as well.

Comment on the illustrations in your books.
A: My books are not for young children, so other than dingbats, no illustrations were made.

Have you anything to say about the encouragement given by your publisher/others?
A: My publishers have always been encouraging, as far as making slight changes in the line of the story went. Copy editors, too, have been very enthusiastic and excited about my books – so far!

Can authors dispel misconceptions, for example prejudices against animals eg."blind as a bat"?
A: As an author, writing for both younger readers of 7 – 9 years, and older ones of 10 – 14 years, I abhor the preachy simplistic attitude of some books here. We must graduate from the teaching/preachiness of talking down to our readers, to treating them like sensible young people, who have a right to opinions of their own, and only need a few good 'directions' to steer them on the right path, leaving the rest to their own powers of reasoning.

In your opinion, is ecology and the natural environment adequately represented in fiction for children and young adults in India? Can more be done?
A: Rural and forest environment is, but there is little on our indigenous peoples, and very little on urban environment stories for very young readers of 5 – 9 years. Especially in local languages. Every rural family has the right to try to attempt to improve their living standards – which often means moving to the city, but rarely does one realize the trials of living in such an environment mean – smaller tin shack homes, little water or light, no space, little privacy, much noise, pollution in noise and air and water…. These could be brought out too, but in a humourous way.

Can more be done? Have you, personally, any plans?

A: I would be happy to, but need funding first. If there are publishers who want such material, and accept proposals, for a regular sum, we can work out something for sure.

Please give us your opinions/suggestions

A: As mentioned above, publishers are in plenty. Why do they wait for manuscripts to be sent to them? Why not put out ads/requirements in relevant newspapers, etc, so potential writers can respond? There should be plenty who would be able to churn out a lot of good written material fitting their requirements?

QUESTIONS TO YA AUTHORS

The youth of today can play a crucial role in averting ecological disaster.

Yet one does not find much about the environment in Young Adult fiction. Please comment.

A: YA readers do not want material which either teaches or preaches! If authors could write about ecological disasters in a fictionalized form, through imaginary protagonists, who face some challenging situations, perhaps readers may be interested. I think majority prefer Fantasy or Adventure fiction.

As an author of young adult fiction, how have you represented nature, ecology, eco-friendly practices, etc. in your books?

A: I have represented the above subjects in as subtle a way as possible. For the reasons as mentioned in the answer above.

If your protagonists are involved with nature, are they passive observers or activists.

A: Passive.

Have you tried to bring in the love of nature in your fiction?

A: Yes, in all my books, I have tried to make this very clear.

Does ya fiction pander to the dreams of westernized, urbanized youth?

A: Definitely. Greatly influenced by Book shop displayed books....Our own publishers and book sellers are to blame for this. They hardly encourage Indian authors (this they're only just beginning to do, I notice with some relief!). Two reasons for this: i) Parents chose the books for their younger children, they rarely allow their kids to chose their own. Big mistake in my opinion! And ii) Young parents recall only their own kid lit – Enid Blyton,

Roald Dahl, Geronimo, Princess Diaries, etc, all foreign authors, tried and tested, selling without publicity, so why spend time and effort on our Indian authors, when this is so much easier? iii) Hence the pandering to misguided dreams of our urban westernized youth.

What can authors do to remind youth of their responsibilities regarding the environment?
A: Write better and more urban outdoor and nature based material. Fiction of course!

Many authors and illustrators (or both) are lovers or nature. Some are conservationists, wildlife photographers, etc. Please share with us some of your experiences.
A: As given in the first Questionnaire.

Please give your suggestions/comments.
A: As given in the first Questionnaire.

Leela Gour Broome
Author: FLUTE IN THE FOREST . (Penguin Puffin 2010.)
RED KITE ADVENTURE   (Penguin Random House 2016.)
THE ANAISHOLA CHRONICLE. (Notion Press 2019.)
(all available on Amazon)

**

SREEKUMAR VARMA

Shreekumar Varma is an author, playwright, newspaper columnist and poet, known for the chidren's novels *Lament of Mohini* (Penguin, 2000), *Maria's Room* (Harper Collins, 2010), *Devil's Garden: Tales Of Pappudom* (Puffin, 2006), *The Magic Store of Nu-Cham-Vu* (Puffin, 2009) and the historical book for children, *Pazhassi Raja: The Royal Rebel* (Macmillan, 1997). Born as HH Prince Punartham Thirunal of the Travancore Royal Family, he is the great great grandson of the artist Raja Ravi Varma and grandson of Regent Maharani Sethu Lakshmi Bayi, the last ruling Maharani of Travancore. He retired as Professor of English at the Madras Christian College.

Sreekumar Varma Interviewed by Dr.GMahendranath, on my behalf:

GM: Though environmental education is part of the curriculum of schools, fiction can play a vital role in imparting ecological values. Do you agree? If yes, please explicate.
SV: I believe that anything that is told in the form of a story or in theatre form comes easier to the children. Always narrate in the form of a story. Children find it easier.
GM: Many authors and illustrators (or both) are lovers or nature. Some are conservationists, wildlife photographers, etc. Please share with us some of your experiences.
SV: I am a lover of nature. I take some time off and go to the mountains or the sea. I am not passionately into ecology or going and sitting down with the animals. Till now I have not done this.
GM: Love of nature automatically brings about understanding and awareness. Do your stories have nature as their background?
SV: In fact, one of my children's novels, *Devil's Garden*, one part is set in the forest. Of course it is a fantasy and animals mutate into other creatures.
 Description of nature is part of my books. In *Lament of Mohini*, the sea is a presence. It is almost a character in the story. Rain, huge, heavy rain serves an important role. In fact, there are one or two pages spent in describing the rain.

GM: What effect does nature have on the character of your protagonists?
SV: Nature does have a presence. Do the characters reflect it? It depends. Mostly as a presence.
GM: Do the children in your books behave in an eco-friendly manner?
SV: If I 'make' them love nature, that means I control them. I never control a character. Each character has his or her own role to play. Mostly friendly towards nature. They don't specifically love nature. They don't even reflect what I think.
GM: What is their attitude to the conservation and pollution?
SV: What is my attitude towards conservation and pollution? I have never done anything specific.
GM: Are they activists or passive observers?
SV: Not passive. Basically active. Activists, mostly. They are not passive observers. There is a message. What we do to nature affects what happens to us. How reaction to nature reflects upon what you get finally.
GM: What is the "message' of your books regarding environmental problems, dilemmas and solutions?
SV: No 'message." What happens to the forests determines what happens to you as well. Your reaction to nature counts.
GM: Are animals portrayed in a realistic and healthy manner?
SV: No, not realistic. Fantasies. Not too much realism. But healthy, I ways, I suppose.
GM: Comment on the relationship of your protagonists to the flora and fauna of their land.
SV: They love it, especially the younger ones. Forests, mountains, the sea. These are the areas I have spoken of, over the years.
GM: What is your relationship with nature. Has nature played an important role in your life?
SV: To a certain extent. The more you are receptive to nature, the more you respond to nature, the healthier you are. I think everyone has a natural rhythm to their lives. I think we are used to. This is what we should teach children - "Back to the earth." When we were children, we used to play outside-we didn't have television or any other electronic items or movies or anything. It was either

reading, which made you think or playing around in the garden, which made you observe and do your own thinking, not what others made you think. In that way you could learn from life. Back to nature, when you are in touch with the earth, you learn more things, Like the seasonal changes or how the animals and birds behave.

GM: What is the "message' of your books regarding environmental problems, dilemmas and solutions?

SV: Now we are stuck in a room with a small screen and that is your relationship with anything. In that way we have actually lost touch with nature. In one of my children's poems published with Penguin (my children's publisher is Penguin), one of the poems is called "The Cyber River" which shows how we lose touch with nature.

GM: Do you adopt a positive approach to the traditional way of life, especially the lives of traditional communities?

SV: Too much tradition is not practical. If you reject everything modern, that is another thing. I write on a laptop. You need not reject electronic goods. But do not depend on them to lead your life. You can make use of the accessories you need, but don't depend upon them to live your life. Nowadays what happens is, if you see something passing by, you don't take note of it; but if you see it on TV, you pay attention. So don't rely too much on either tradition or modernity. You don't have to lead a very rigid or ascetic life.

GM: How do you work in tandem with your illustrator to project your ideas?

Comment on the illustrations in your books.

SV: Two of my books were very easy because the illustrator was my own son [Vinayak Varma]. He is also a writer and illustrator. He worked for Amar Chitra Katha as Art Director for their magazine. So he worked on mine – on two of my books. *The Magic Store of Num Cham Wu* and *Maria's Room*. I gave him an idea. I described it. It was difficult because it was a fantasy. But he did a good job of it and the publisher had good words for his work. I love it since it is the work of my own son.

GM: Have you anything to say about the encouragement given by your publisher/others?

SV: My publishers have stuck by me. Penguin has been my children's publisher. For my books for adults, I have moved from Macmillan to Penguin to HarpeCollins. It depends on the editor. When they move, they ask us to come. On the whole, they have been supportive and encouraging. I am happy with my publishers.

GM: Can authors dispel misconceptions, for example prejudices against animals eg."blind as a bat"?

SV: This is not very practical to do. For example, if we take away everything referring to animals which we have grown used with, just because we think it will hurt animals. I told this in front of blind people, who refer to themselves as blind. It is our attitude that counts, not politically correct terms. Two of my books, *Maria's Room* and *Wun Chan Wu* are available is audio versions for the blind. I insisted on that, there should be two versions, one print and another audio.

GM: In your opinion, is ecology and the natural environment adequately represented in fiction for children and young adults in India?

SV: I think more and more young publishers are coming out with these things. Specifically and purposefully coming out. Their publications are educational and entertaining, bringing out ore stories related to this. I don't know if adequately.

GM: Can more be done? Have you, personally, any plans?

SV: I have personally no plans. I am sure that there are many people who love nature and ecological balance so much that they will promote these things, but in my case, I just write stories, depending on my preferences and the preferences of my characters regarding the things they will come out. But I don't go about specifically having an agenda about these things.

GM: Please give us your opinions/suggestions

SV: Like I said, children have to be made aware. They have to go out to the ground. That habit must be inculcated in children. People live in flats. Children come down, play, go back to the television and the computer. It depends to a large extent on the determination of parents and teachers. Take them to green areas, forest bodies. It should be a happy sort of thing, not part of their creative work.

It is convenient for parents to make the children sit in front of computers. You lose vision, memory, thinking capacity. A computer is a tool. Life is a much bigger thing Can't conjure up life into a small screen.

First of all, discover life for yourselves, not through the Internet. Observe first-hand, the Internet will teach you more afterwards. Go out and experiment. Develop sympathy, empathy, understanding of older people and people different from you with regard to caste, community language. We lead cloistered existences.

I teach children, too. It is the stage when they are the most creative. Parents should give them more freedom. They should remember their own childhoods and become one with the children. I had the opportunity of playing in a big compound, with trees and other children.

GM: Have you been inspired by anyone to write?

SV: I was not inspired by anyone specific to write. I have been a story-teller since childhood. Telling stories came naturally to me. I have been a journalist, run my own business, then become a writer in 2000. But I have written plays before. My plays greatly outnumber my stores. I was writing even in 1986, when I was doing business.

GM: Thank you, Sir, for the long interview.

SV: It was a pleasure meeting you, young man! All the best for the project!

SANDHYA RAO

Sandhya Rao, profilic author of children's fiction, was former senior Editor at Tulika Publishers. One of the finest writers for children in India today, her books have won awards and accolades: *My Friend the Sea* won the Ambitious Children's Book Project award at the Berlin Children and Youth Literature Festival, 2005. My Mother's Sari was chosen as an Outstanding International Book, 2007, by the United States Board for Books for Young People (USBBY) and the Children's Book Council. Rights to the book have been sold for USA, Canada and other countries.

QUESTIONS TO AUTHORS OF CHILDREN'S FICTION

Though environmental education is part of the curriculum of schools, fiction can play a vital role in imparting ecological values. Do you agree? If yes, please explicate.

Definitely it can. Children usually read with belief.... They always ask: Is this real? Did this really happen?

Many authors and illustrators (or both) are lovers or nature. Some are conservationists, wildlife photographers, etc. Please share with us some of your experiences.

Is that right? I didn't know that. But I do understand that children are naturally fascinated by nature. When they are little, because of their small size, they notice all the small things. When my son was a toddler, the thing closest to him was the ground. So he'd always be bent over noticing every blade of grass, every piece of 'shit' (literally)... and he'd be full of questions: can we eat it? Can we drink it? Etc etc Another time after a heavy shower, our tiny lawn was overrun with slugs. He just happily began picking them up. My nephew would pick up lizards from the wall and throw them out into the garden to oblige his grandmother. Whenever my dad took us on car rides, he would stop and make us look at trees and leaves and vegetables. I remember how he pulled out peanuts from the ground and showed us how they grew.

Love of nature automatically brings about understanding and awareness. Do your stories have nature as their background?

Have responded to this earlier. Yes, always. We live in nature, so you don't have to make an extra effort to introduce nature. It's seamless.

What effect does nature have on the character of your protagonists?

That depends, really. But certainly the protagonists will always react to nature, in whatever way. Literally or figuratively.

Do the children in your books behave in an eco-friendly manner?
What is their attitude to the conservation and pollution?
Are they activists or passive observers?
What is the "message' of your books regarding environmental problems, dilemmas and solutions?

To answer in a general way to all these questions: it rather depends upon the story and the characters. To make them behave artificially simply to make a point defeats the purpose of being a writer I think. In any case, however it is conveyed, a good writer will always get the right message across.

I will take the liberty of answering generally, okay? It's great to be able to work closely with illustrators, but not always possible. But certainly one makes suggestions. And yes, we need to be careful to dispel false notions.... Sometimes these things happen owing to lack of knowledge. For instance, in one story, Crocodile Tears, we tried to make the Snake a sensitive soul, a small effort at winning friends for this largely unfriended creature.
I think one should just keep writing from the heart. Children listen, they read with their hearts, they read with emotion, even teenagers. So we should just keep doing it for them.

Dr. GRAEME MACQEEN-CANADA

Graeme MacQueen received his Ph.D. in Buddhist Studies from Harvard University and taught in the Religious Studies Department of McMaster University for 30 years. While at McMaster he became founding Director of the Centre for Peace Studies at McMaster, after which he helped develop the B.A. program in Peace Studies and oversaw the development of peace-building projects in Sri Lanka, Gaza, Croatia and Afghanistan. Graeme was a member of the organizing committee of the Toronto Hearings held on the 10th anniversary of 9/11 and is co-editor of The Journal of 9/11 Studies. His fascination with India and the Buddhist faith resulted in the young adult book, *Journey to the City of the Six Gates*.

To
macqueen@mcmaster.ca
11 Nov
Dear   Sir,
I greatly enjoyed and appreciated your most unusual book, published by Tulika.

I teach English Literature at a college in India. I am doing a research project on the representation of Ecology and the natural environment as represented in English language fiction for children and young adults published in India.

I found your book highly relevant to my area and have included it in my report to be sent to the funding agency next month. I hope to present a paper, too on it soon.

Could you share with me some of the thoughts that led to your writing this book? What is the relationship between man and nature that you wish to express? Spirituality seems to be the link.

I am also particularly happy and at the same time curious that you have chosen to portray Indian characters. (I asked the same question to Mr.Ken Spillman, who is Australian). I suppose that it is your interest in Buddhism that has led to such a natural portrayal,Sir.I read that theSix Gates are stages of spiritual development.

I am very much attracted to the journey motif. I explored it with reference to Tolkien and Rowling, applying some of Jung and Campbell's ideas, in my PhD thesis, 'Archetypes in Fantasy Fiction: A study of J.R,R.Tolkien and J.K.Rowling,'available as a free resource online. (www.languageinindia.com). I would like to see if Campbell's stages can be identified in Six Gates.

Looking forward to your reply,
Yours sincerely,
Shobha

Graeme MacQueen
To
me
11 Nov
Dear Dr. Ramaswamy:

What a wonderful surprise to get your email message! When I wrote *Journey* I became fully caught up in the characters and the story. But it is some years ago now and I tend to assume no one reads the book anymore, and I tend to think Mati and Satya live only in my mind. How nice to think that someone, especially someone in India, will be honouring them with research and reflection.

I should begin by saying that I don't think authors should be the interpreters of their works or that they should hover over their works shooing away interpretations they don't agree with or haven't thought of. After all, I was the conduit for the story, but now it belongs, for better or worse, to everyone—even the trees. I suppose I'm being playful but I'm also being serious. I hate it when authors of literary works tell us how to read what they've written.

In short, you have free rein to make what you will of the novel. I will just make a few comments—and even these are probably too many!

First, it would be true to say that there's a connection between my work in Buddhism and the novel. But it's a connection that goes deep to the heart of things and is not merely intellectual. I began my relationship to Buddhism when I was 18 years old (perhaps even a bit earlier), and when we are that age we are still in the process of development as human beings. So my relationship to that tradition goes very deep and was never a mainly intellectual pursuit.

Academic research can be quite dry, but at times I managed to find a way to deal with the themes that really interested me. Here is an example:

http://blogs.dickinson.edu/buddhistethics/files/2010/04/macqu021.pdf

When it came to writing the novel, I was able to cast off the pretence of objectivity and speak from a deeper place. I recall weeping as I wrote some sections of the book. I suppose that isn't unusual for authors, but in any case it is worth mentioning.

As for India and its stories, India is such a repository of stories, such a tremendous source of narrative, that at one point in the 19th century (I don't recall the details) one European academic came up with the theory that all folk tales originally came from India! Of course, he was wrong—all peoples have the capacity for narrative—but this was a sign of how deeply Europeans had been impressed when they studied the world's tales and found so many of them could be traced back to India. During my academic career I read hundreds and hundreds of Indian stories, including all of the roughly 500 jataka tales. I studied Pali and Sanskrit and even Chinese (the Chinese translated many of these Indian stores centuries ago) to have access to the originals. So when it came to writing a story of my own the motifs from ancient India came to me quite naturally.

I had become involved a few years before writing *Journey* in contributing to a collection of tales published under the editorship of Griffin Ondaatje as *The Monkey King*. You can probably find a copy somewhere. And then I discovered, to my delight, that one of the tales in that collection (a Buddhist tale retold by me as "Brighter Still") had been included, in an edited form, in the *The New Gul Mohar Graded English Course*, Reader 6. In this way, students in India would be learning to read English with the help of this little Buddhist tale. When I wrote to Orient Longman to thank them a very nice woman there encouraged me to write a full novel for young people in India. So I did. That is how *Journey* came about. When Orient Longman phased out that part of their publication series, I found a home for the MS at Tulika. Tulika was just the right place—a publishing company that seemed to be run by women who wanted books with positive role models for girls and who were very sympathetic to tales that encouraged reverence for the natural world.

The last thing I will say is that India has many Matis at the moment who are great activists and great defenders of nature and of the poor. I immediately think of two that I have met: Vandana Shiva and Medha Patkar. They definitely inspired me. Later, I became involved in the early stages of the Mahila Shanti Sena, a movement for the rights of women that started in Bihar several years ago.

I fear I've said too much already. I must leave the interpretation job to you...

Oh, one last comment. I certainly read *Lord of the Rings* years ago and loved it but I purposely did not read any of Rowling's works. I was afraid I would be too readily influenced and might produce a poor copy.

All the best, and by all means write if you have further questions.

Graeme

Graeme MacQueen
To
me
11 Nov
Dear Shobha: I was thinking after I sent my reply that there is so much I've left out. Let me just mention one thing that is too important to omit. When I was young I read *The Jungle Book* by Kipling and was entranced by it. So if someone sees hints of Mowgli in *Journey* that's no surprise, although I certainly did not write explicitly with that in mind. Kipling is often denounced these days as an imperialist and a racist, and I dare say that's all true, but he was also a supreme writer of English (unfortunately those two sets of characteristics are not mutually exclusive). His clean, strong prose and his ability to make us believe his nonhuman creatures when they speak still amaze me.

All the best,

Graeme

KEN SPILLMAN, Australia

Ken Spillman is one of Australia's most versatile and prolific authors, editors and critics. He is the author of more than 35 books spanning many genres. He spends around half of his time travelling and has a special fondness for India, the setting for several of his books. He has been published and widely read in the country, hence his inclusion in the study. His Advaita the Writer, published by Tulika is set in a boarding school in India. His Daydreamer Dev series has an Indian boy experience adventure in various natural surroundings all over the world and is informative as well as entertaining. Ken Spillman is a member of the board of the Asian Festival of Children's Content, and chairs the judging panel for Singapore's first major award for children's literature. His official website is www.kenspillman.com.

Dear Shobha,

Thank you for your email. I have been wracking my brain, trying to think of when I received some questions that I have not yet answered. Although I do try to keep up with the emails and requests I get, something must have gone wrong, because I cannot recall the eco question you have referred to.

Perhaps you could send them again?

Thank you so much for your comments regarding 'Radhika takes the Plunge'. I enjoyed writing that book and have commenced another Radhika book this year.

Why do I often write about Indians? Well, I didn't plan to, but from the time I first visited India I have continued to get ideas that seem to involve Indian characters. I'm sure that visiting India 2-3 times a year keeps those ideas coming, and the fact that I love to read Indian fiction also helps. The bottom line? I love India!

Warm regards,
Ken

Ken Spillman

Web: www.kenspillman.com
Twitter: @kenspillmansays
Facebook: ken.spillman.9

Mon, 22 Jul 2013 at 11:25
Mon, 11:25
Message starred

Re: enjoyed Radhika's plunge

- *Ken Spillman*
-

ToShobha Ramaswamy
Hi Shobha,
I have jotted some replies in red below.
Hope this helps!
With best wishes

Ken

Ken Spillman

Web: www.kenspillman.com
Twitter: @kenspillmansays
Facebook: ken.spillman.9

On 22 July 2013 01:49, Shobha Ramaswamy <shobini_2005@yahoo.co.in> wrote:

Dear Sir,
I have a terrible number of questions, but I think You may find them rather tiresome. So, I will shorten them. Please tell me whether you feel that fiction can instil ecological values and eco friendly behaviour pattern in children and young adults.

Reading fiction will always lead to a deeper understanding of the world, and broader interests. Therefore it may promote an appreciation of social and natural environments - so yes, it CAN instil those values but may not always.

Many children's writers have a special relationship with nature. They may be wildlife photographers, artists, etc. Can you share with us some of your experiences?

Being observant is part and parcel of being a writer. Being observant also increases our appreciation of beauty - and writers also need to reflect on experience and observation, often in tranquil places. I think this is all true for me. As a teenager I used to sit for many hours watching the waves at a nearby beach, just being absorbed by their patterns and sounds. All through my life I have felt more 'at peace' in nature - among trees, birds etc. The creative mind needs space, and nature gives it the space to do the necessary processing of things.

What is the role of nature in your books? Do many of them have nature as a background?

This really depends on the story. The story comes first, and when nature can play a part in the story I use it. For example, Scholastic India will this year be publishing a novel for teens that I wrote. In that story, screeching parrots are observed by the character and he makes up a whole imaginative, funny story about parrots.

Do your protagonists encounter ecological /environmental issues? What do they do? Are they activists or passive witnesses?

This is not really relevant to my fiction - except for incidents like the above, and Daydreamer Dev (see below)

Do the children in your books have a special relationship with nature? Are they influenced by the setting/background?

All children are influenced by their settings, and my characters are no exception. In my Daydreamer Dev series, Dev is 'transported' to natural settings - the Amazon River, Mount Everest, the Sahara - and he needs to engage with it at a personal level. Even though the series is for kids, Dev always emerges with a deeper understanding and appreciation of these settings. The stories parallel the process of learning about environments through books, study, the Internet, because through an imagined adventure, Dev acquires 'virtual' experience.

Any comments, suggestions, anything else you would like to share? What about India, Indian children and your experiences here?

Well, I love India and have been influenced by it to such an extent that I now write about Indian characters and settings. It stimulates my imagination!

From: Ken Spillman <kenspillman@gmail.com>;
To: Shobha Ramaswamy <shobini_2005@yahoo.co.in>;
Subject: Re: enjoyed Radhika's plunge
Sent: Fri, Jul 19, 2013 7:01:49 AM

Radhika's plunge

- Ken Spillman

To

Shobha Ramaswamy

Dear Shobha,
I am not sure how I managed to forget this, but I wrote another book with clear environmental themes. It is called Magpie Mischief: An Amity Kids Adventure. This book is about a 'gang' of kids who have made friends with the magpies at their school. During nesting season, the magpies have a habit of swooping at children to warn them to keep away from their nests - but they don't swoop the kids who have made friends with them. When there is a move to get rid of the magpies, the children need to take action and they come up with an alternative solution to the swooping issue. This story acknowledges that the Australian magpie is a native bird - and a beautiful, intelligent one at that. The message is that we need to use our brains and find ways of living with them - instead of destroying/dominating them. The book won an Environment

Award from the Wilderness Society. It's available now as an ebook on Amazon.com.
My apologies for forgetting about this earlier!!
Ken

Ken Spillman

Web: www.kenspillman.com
Twitter: @kenspillmansays
Facebook: ken.spillman.9

On 22 July 2013 22:59, Shobha Ramaswamy <shobini_2005@yahoo.co.in> wrote:
Thank you very much, Sir for your detailed and thought-provoking replies to my queries. It was really nice of you to share your seaside observations. Being an Australian, I think the sea is close to your heart, Sir!
I liked the Daydreamer series - I read the one about the Amazon and the one about the Himalayas. I'm looking forward to the Scholastic release.
Thank you once again for helping out with my project.
Yours faithfully,
Shobha

ANUSHKA RAVISHANKAR

Anushka Ravishankar, a mathematics graduate, has made a name for herself internationally as an Indian children's writer, with over 10 books of verse, fiction and non-fiction. Her special talent is in the area of nonsense verse, where she brilliantly adapts this difficult genre to Indian English usage, without a false note. She has written extensively for Tara Books and other publishers, and is present publisher, along with Sayoni Basu, of Duckbill Books. She has also been Associate Editor of Scholastic India. From Alphabets are Amazing *Animals* to *Excuse Me, Is This India?* and *The Tiger on a Tree*, Ravishankar's books of nonsense verse have become popular with several generations of children. With 17 children's books to her credit, Ravishankar is among the best known Indian children's writers in the business. It is to be noted that she started writing because she was appalled by the dearth of children's books published in India. She is also the Co-founder, Editor and Publisher of Duckbill Books.

Dear Anushka,
Please, could you write a few lines about what Duckbill and the children's book publishing scenario in India, esp. With regard to books projecting nature and Eco issues and those with nature as background?
Many children's authors share a special relationship with nature. They may be photographers, artists, etc. Can you share with us some of your experiences?

Any other comments, suggestions are most welcome.
Yours hopefully,
Shobha

Dear Shobha

I don't think I have a more special relationship with nature than anyone else. I also think it's unfair to say that only those who are artists and photographers share a special relationship with nature. What about gardeners? And it also depends on what you mean by nature. Doesn't nature include the wind and the rain and clouds and the sea? And what about animals? So I think a lot of people have special relationships with nature - from sailors to veterinarians.

In the same way, a book doesn't have to be *about* an eco issue to be eco-sensitive. Duckbill, as publishers, and I, as an author, firmly believe that these issues have to inform our stories subtly. So we make sure our stories contain kindness to animals, sensitivity to the environment and gender sensitivity, without stating or making a didactic point of any of these things.

Having said that, there are publishers who do this overtly, and some of them are doing a great job of it - like the books by TERI, some of the early books of Tara Publishing, some books by Tulika. These are the ones I'm aware of; I'm sure there are more.

I do hope this has helped.

Best wishes
Anushka

Anushka Ravishankar
Duckbill Books

www.duckbill.in

Dear Shobha

I forgot to apologise in my last mail for not responding to your questionnaire and reminder. I'm really sorry - we've been very swamped.

And I thought I'd add this about the portrayal of animals in books: at Duckbill, we're a little prejudiced against anthropomorphic animals. While there have been some brilliant books and films that do this well, there are many more that do this very badly indeed! Essentially, putting animals in clothes and making them behave exactly like humans is something that bothers us deeply.

I was looking at your questionnarie, and I think what I said earlier pretty much answers these questions: if we as authors or publishers are sensitive to ecological concerns, we will do books where the protagonists are eco-sensitive and care about animals and nature, without using every book as an opportunity to hit children over the head with lessons on environment and ecology. :)

Do let me know if there are any more specific questions you'd like me to answer - either as publisher or as author.

Apologies again, and thank you for being so patient!

Regards
Anushka

On 22 July 2013 09:01, Anushka Ravishankar <anushka@duckbill.in> wrote:

ASHA NEHEMIAH

Asha Nehemiah writes books for children from 3-12, where wonderfully funny characters get into crazy adventures. Her books for children have been translated into Hindi, Tamil, Bengali, Assamese and Urdu. Her books include *Granny's Sari, The Rajah's Moustache*, *The Mystery of the Secret Hair Oil Formula*, *The Mystery of the Silk Umbrella*, and *Meddling Mooli and the Blue-Legged Alien*.

QUESTIONS TO AUTHORS OF CHILDREN'S FICTION

Ques: *Though environmental education is part of the curriculum of schools, fiction can play a vital role in imparting ecological values. Do you agree? If yes, please explicate.*

Ans: I would say fiction can play an important role in sensitizing children to ecological issues. Fiction can provide a platform for discussion in the classroom and informally among groups of children. Fiction can make children question and think. I'm not sure we should look to fiction to impart values.

Ques: *Many authors and illustratriors (or both) are lovers or nature. Some are conservationists, wildlife photographers, etc. Please share with us some of your experiences.*

Ans: ----------------

Ques: Love of nature automatically brings about understanding and awareness. Do your stories have nature as their background?

Ans: **NO, my stories do not have nature as background.**

Ques: What effect does nature have on the character of your protagonists?

Can more be done? Have you, personally, any plans?

Please give us your opinions/suggestions

ANS: **Shoba, I'm afraid I'm not all the right person to answer these questions as Nature, Environment and Ecology do not play a significant role in my fiction. Since I have nothing of value to add, please excuse me from answering these questions.**

HARINI GOPALSWAMI SREENIVASAN

Harini Gopalswami Srinivasan is an established author of children's fiction. She has written : Zoo Duck, an award-winning picture book published by the Children's Book Trust, and *The Smile of Vanuvati*, a historical adventure published by Tulika Books, besides *Gind*, a book focusing on ecology with a mythological background. A nomad at heart, Harini has lived all over India. She is presently based in Bangalore with her husband and two daughters.

QUESTIONS TO AUTHORS OF CHILDREN'S FICTION
-Harini Gopalswami Sreenivasan

Though environmental education is part of the curriculum of schools, fiction can play a vital role in imparting ecological values. Do you agree? If yes, please explicate.
Yes, but not fiction-with-an-agenda. Values – ecological and otherwise – are a part of the author's world view that come through in the story. Plot and characters should not be subservient to external considerations like conveying a

message, but should develop according to their own internal logic.

Many authors and illustrators (or both) are lovers or nature. Some are conservationists, wildlife photographers, etc. Please share with us some of your experiences.

Writers and artists are supposed to observe the world around them and process what they observe in their own way, which results in a creative output. If we fulfill this function, our observation of nature almost inevitably leads to a sense of wonder, not unlike love.

Speaking personally, I am not naturally observant, though I have tried to develop this faculty. But I have always loved nature and animals and I think this does come through in my writing. I could never think of writing a book about (or living in) an entirely human/ urban community, with no animals to enliven it!

Love of nature automatically brings about understanding and awareness. Do your stories have nature as their background?

I'm not sure. I think perhaps my love of nature is conveyed in some way to the reader, but the story is the main thing.

What effect does nature have on the character of your protagonists?

My protagonists tend to be nature-lovers. Maybe they take nature for granted, as many of us do. In my most recent book, *Gind*, the protagonist is a vanara, a child of the forest, at a time when there were no concerns about ecology. Hopefully his familiarity with, and affection for, the forest and its denizens will rub off on readers. In *Zoo Duck*, the naturalist is the secondary hero, after the duck and his friends!

Do the children in your books behave in an eco-friendly manner?

Not specifically, but they don't behave in a non-eco-friendly manner.

What is their attitude to the conservation and pollution? Are they activists or passive observers?

They are not activists, and the issue of conservation is never brought up, but the underlying assumption is that they care.
What is the "message' of your books regarding environmental problems, dilemmas and solutions?
The only message is that one should care – about this wonderful world and every creature and natural phenomenon to be found in it.
Are animals portrayed in a realistic and healthy manner?
I think healthy, but am not so sure about realistic.
Comment on the relationship of your protagonists to the flora and fauna of their land.
Some of my protagonists *are* fauna of their land, the others have an easy and friendly relationship with other living beings.
Do you adopt a positive approach to the traditional way of life, especially the lives of traditional communities?
Yes, very much. In *The Smile of Vanuvati*, the portrayal of the villager Bholu's life shows that, along with great hardship, there is still plenty of opportunity for satisfaction, friendship and happiness. Similarly, the characters in *Gind* demonstrate that simplicity and happiness often go hand in hand, and that high spirits and good humour are more important than material possessions.
How do you work in tandem with your illustrator to project your ideas? Comment on the illustrations in your books.
This is rather a sore point, so please don't quote me! I have to say that Indian publishers don't give authors much say in the way their work is illustrated. In the case of *Zoo Duck*, the first I knew about its publication was when ten copies landed up on my doorstep! However, I am very happy with the illustrator they chose and love her artwork! The cover of *The Smile of Vanuvati* too is quite appropriate, though I had something more mysterious in mind and would have liked to be consulted. In the case of *Gind*, I had quite heated arguments with the publishers. I wanted the book to be pitched as a fantasy, which would have to be represented by a quite different kind of cover. I even made them a collage of various pictures that created the effect I wanted, but the marketing dept insisted on

pitching it as a traditional epic-based story. They finally overrode my wishes and came out with an Amar Chitra Katha-like cover. I still think that was a big mistake and killed its chances of reaching the readership that it was aimed at.

Have you anything to say about the encouragement given by your publisher/others?

I'm truly grateful to the editors who saw something in my work and gave me a chance.

At the moment, however, I have at least three unpublished manuscripts doing the rounds, which several publishers have turned down as 'good, but won't sell'. I think publishers should think of developing public taste as part of their job, take a chance on what they think is good and then push it enthusiastically. Instead they are slaves to the market, and there is a flattening of the variety of books being published and, therefore, read.

Can authors dispel misconceptions, for example prejudices against animals eg."blind as a bat"?

Definitely, but it is only incidental to the story!

In your opinion, is ecology and the natural environment adequately represented in fiction for children and young adults in India?

There just isn't enough children's and YA fiction being published in India! Given that – yes, I think a lot of writers and illustrators are portraying the environment sensitively and arguing the case for conservation persuasively. For younger children, I've seen some really great picture books by Tulika, Tara and CBT, among others.

Can more be done? Have you, personally, any plans?

Read, write and publish more!

Please give us your opinions/suggestions.

I'd really like to see the children's publishing industry in India pull up its socks and put in place support systems for improving the quality of our books: literary agencies that take an active interest in what is published and not only place manuscripts but also help writers polish their work; commissioning editors with vision and the guts to **realize that**

vision; marketing people who love books and not just the money they could make on them; more focus on work and less on people.

RADHA H.S

Radha HS is primarily a children's author based in Bangalore, who writes stories, rebus stories, science and craft pieces, games, and plays for children of all ages. Besides picture and puzzle books, her work has been published in magazines within India and outside. She has also illustrated some of her books. She designs/creates puzzles for both children and grownups.

QUESTIONS TO AUTHORS OF CHILDREN'S FICTION

Though environmental education is part of the curriculum of schools, fiction can play a vital role in imparting ecological values. Do you agree? If yes, please explicate.
I do agree. Learning about most things via a story embellished with illustrations is absorbed without going through the 'learning' which happens in curriculum based study.
Many authors and illustrators (or both) are lovers or nature. Some are conservationists, wildlife photographers, etc. Please share with us some of your experiences.
The first time I observed a mud dauber build its home, stock it, seal it and disappear, my personal curiosity had made me take pictures and read up about them. Also, I was curious to know what their 'English' name was. The same happened with weaver ants which were all over our trees in Mysore. I wrote

about both creatures. When paper wasps built their nests and I saw complete destruction by a hornet, I took pictures again. I learnt about urban wildlife and I had an urge to share their story. So I wrote.

Love of nature automatically brings about understanding and awareness. Do your stories have nature as their background?
Some have.

What effect does nature have on the character of your protagonists?
I have generally used nature to stage a situation.

Do the children in your books behave in an eco-friendly manner?
In my books I have incorporated Nature and my characters are a part of nature's cycle.

What is their attitude to the conservation and pollution?
I have written picture books and puzzle books. My characters try to convey the hazards of not conserving.

Are they activists or passive observers?
They participate.

What is the "message' of your books regarding environmental problems, dilemmas and solutions?
Do not mess up Nature or she'll mess with you.

Are animals portrayed in a realistic and healthy manner?
I think so.

Comment on the relationship of your protagonists to the flora and fauna of their land.
My protagonists participate in the cycle of life. E.g. The ant in my book carries seeds home which grow into trees from which fruits and flowers grow.

Do you adopt a positive approach to the traditional way of life, especially the lives of traditional communities?
I try. Like the lives of the Irula I wrote about for a newspaper - their snake catching abilities are still relevant today, but the people want to be mainstreamed and want to do other things. People adapt and adopt new lifestyles.

How do you work in tandem with your illustrator to project your ideas?

For some books I am not at all involved. For others, I give suggested drawings. Occasionally I have had to ask for a slight change in illustration.
*Comment on the illustrations in your **books**.*
I like some better than others.
Have you anything to say about the encouragement given by your publisher/others?
Most useful.
Can authors dispel misconceptions, for example prejudices against animals eg."blind as a bat"?
Author's can try more than others.
In your opinion, is ecology and the natural environment adequately represented in fiction for children and young adults in India?
No.
Can more be done? Have you, personally, any plans?
I am sure a larger body of work can be created. I have no plans at the moment.
Please give us your opinions/suggestions
The Indian picture book market is very small for the population we have.

SOWMYA RAJENDRAN

Sowmya Rajendran has published many books with Tulika – *Aana and Chena*, *The Snow King's Daughter*, *Power Cut*, *School is Cool* and *Mayil Will Not Be Quiet*. She has also contributed a story to the *Water Stories from Around the World* anthology. Sowmya enjoys writing for children and believes in creating work that encourages them to explore the world from multiple perspectives. She previously worked with Chandamama, the children's magazine. *Monday to Sunday*, a bilingual picture book, is her latest. She frequently collaborates with her friend and fellow-writer, Niveditha Subramaniam. Their *Mayil Will **Not Be Quiet*** is about a teen-aged girl's growing-up experiences and touches on issues of religious, gender and sexual identity, and respecting diversity and equality.

QUESTIONS TO AUTHORS OF CHILDREN'S FICTION

Though environmental education is part of the curriculum of schools, fiction can play a vital role in imparting ecological values. Do you agree? If yes, please explicate.
Yes. When a child studies a lesson, s/he aims to remember it till the exams in most cases. But in the case of fiction which the child voluntarily reads and enjoys, the retention capacity is likely to be higher. Identifying with the characters and the situations described will make it easier for the child to absorb the spirit of the message.
Many authors and illustratiors (or both) are lovers or nature. Some are conservationists, wildlife photographers, etc. Please share with us some of your experiences.
I love visiting wildlife sanctuaries and observing the animals in their natural environment. I also follow eco-friendly practices like separating biodegradable trash from plastics.
Love of nature automatically brings about understanding and awareness. Do your stories have nature as their background?
Well, not specifically though I do try to make my characters environment-friendly.

What effect does nature have on the character of your protagonists?
In Mayil Will Not Be Quiet, a YA novel I co-authored with Niveditha Subramaniam, Mayil develops an environment-friendly game called Paati on Wheels for a contest. It has many rounds that are eco-friendly and talks about environment awareness in a fun way. I've also worked on a soon-to-be-released YA adventure series with Karadi Tales in which one of the adventures is set in a sanctuary in Wayanad and deals with the problem of poaching.
Do the children in your books behave in an eco-friendly manner?
Refer above for this question and the ones below.
What is their attitude to the conservation and pollution?
Are they activists or passive observers?
What is the "message' of your books regarding environmental problems, dilemmas and solutions?
Are animals portrayed in a realistic and healthy manner?
One of the picture books I've written has a talking elephant – I guess that isn't realistic but I think that's all right. Some of the best children's books do have animal characters that aren't always doing realistic things (If You Give a Mouse a Cookie, for instance) and I don't think children get confused because of this.
Comment on the relationship of your protagonists to the flora and fauna of their land.
Do you adopt a positive approach to the traditional way of life, especially the lives of traditional communities?
While I don't believe that there is only one way to live and that modernity is what everyone must adopt, I also think we sometimes exoticize traditional communities and believe that certain people must go on living in their old ways even if they want to change. We tend to see that as saddening. I believe there are positives in all these ways of lives and it is up to individuals what they wish to adopt. If a tribal child wants to go to a city and become a software engineer, Ithink that's okay.
How do you work in tandem with your illustrator to project your ideas?

I sometimes offer visual suggestions if I feel strongly about how something should be depicted, I also go through the illustrations once they are done to make sure they match the text. But beyond this, I don't interfere.
Comment on the illustrations in your books.
I'm happy with them, obviously ☺
Have you anything to say about the encouragement given by your publisher/others?
It's often a talented editor who spots the potential in your manuscript and pushes the idea further. I've been very fortunate to work with such editors at Tulika, Karadi Tales, and Penguin.
Can authors dispel misconceptions, for example prejudices against animals eg."blind as a bat"?
Sure. If you take the Twilight series, it has made vampires really desirable! Though I don't like those books myself, I'm sure a teenager watching a bat fly will be less repulsed and more fascinated by it now! Same with what Harry Potter achieved with owls.
In your opinion, is ecology and the natural environment adequately represented in fiction for children and young adults in India?
I think environment figures largely in many Indian books, especially books for younger children.
Can more be done? Have you, personally, any plans?
Refer reply to environment in my books.

NIVEDITHA SUBRAMANIAM

Niveditha Subramaniam is excited by the possibilities of picture books and comics, and loves photography. She has published several books, including Mayil Will Not Be Quiet (along with her friend and fellow-author, Sowmya Rajendran), Jalebi Curls and The Musical Donkey. She works with Tulika as an editor.

Though environmental education is part of the curriculum of schools, fiction can play a vital role in imparting ecological values. Do you agree? If yes, please explicate.

Yes, definitely. Because in fiction, dry and complex subjects can be addressed imaginatively. Through stories, situations, characters – ecological and environmental issues can be addressed naturally, within the context of the story and can perhaps even give children a more wholistic understanding of real situations. Creative non-fiction works well too.

Any suggestions to improve the questionnaire?

Perhaps it's a bit too specific? Which is not a bad thing, if the people you're sending it out are people who are nature/environment writers, to begin with. A lot of those questions immediately become pertinent.

Though, I *would* suggest rephrasing some of the questions, for instance, the one about featuring eco-friendly children. Maybe you could ask for instances of how child protagonists in fiction first encounter eco-sensitive issues and then how do they tackle them? The interest is always in how the solutions emerge, right? Just my two bit :)

All the best, Niveditha

D.RONALD HADRIAN

Coimbatore--based author of young adult fiction, Ronald Hadrian is a promising writer, who became a published author while still a postgraduate student. He has presently written three books, greatly influenced by the scenic beauty of his native Nilgiris. He teaches at a University in Coimbatore.

QUESTIONS TO AUTHORS OF CHILDREN'S FICTION

Though environmental education is part of the curriculum of schools, fiction can play a vital role in imparting ecological values. Do you agree? If yes, please explicate.

Ans: I absolutely agree. Fiction has the ability to make the most absurdly boring subjects fun. If the students simply learn about ecology without any concern or feeling for the environment then they will simply learn for getting marks. To dramatis any subject with made-up characters will definitely play a vital-role in imparting ecological values.

Many authors and illustratiors (or both) are lovers or nature. Some are conservationists, wildlife photographers, etc. Please share with us some of your experiences.

Ans: I really love nature. I mostly go out for a stroll in the evening, this is the time I get ideas. I live in a hill station, the beautiful tress sway with the wind. It is a beautiful place. But to see people cut tress or build houses in a beautiful lawn it is really depressing.

Love of nature automatically brings about understanding and awareness. Do your stories have nature as their background?

Ans: Yes, sometimes I write, but I am not sure how many people really understand the important point that is made other than the story itself.

In your opinion, is ecology and the natural environment adequately represented in fiction for children and young adults in India?

Ans: Not really. They must be represent it more to have a major impact among children.

QUESTIONS TO YA AUTHORS

The youth of today can play a crucial role in averting ecological disaster.Yet one does not find much about the environment in ya fiction.Please comment.

Ans: Yes certainly, as young adult fiction is primarily for teens, writers tend to write about adventures and young romances to get the attention of young adults. It is true youth can play a major role, but the young must be given the direction and a plan to accomplish anything. They must seriously be educated about the environment and what is happening around them. They must realize there is a big world out there other than the TV and computer.

Have you tried to bring in the love of nature in your fiction?

Not in fiction, but certainly in poetry.

Does ya fiction pander to the dreams of westernized, urbanized youth?

Ans: Yes it does. Young men and women tend to act and behave by what they see and what they hear. Urbanized slang and behaviour is the hot topic in young fiction. This sometimes does not align with the moral values of our culture.

Please give your suggestions/comments.

I am sorry I can't be much help to you in this issue. Whatever I can honestly express I have said. I didn't want to answer any question just for the sake of answering. Thank you. God Bless.

Views of the Illustrators

ASHOK RAJAGOPALAN

Ashok Rajagopalan (also known under the blogging pseudonym Kenny Wordsmith) is a writer and artist for over 500 children's books. Rajagopalan has also worked as a graphic designer, freelance cartoonist, and has contributed to the children's magazines *Impulse Hoot* and *Impulse Toot*. He first began illustrating children's stories with a piece in the 1989 magazine *Junior Quest*. Before working in illustration Rajagopalan received a mechanical engineering diploma and worked as a marketing executive, but found that he disliked the experience. In 2011 he participated in a Kickstarter campaign to fund a comic he was co-creating with the artist Asvin Srivatsangam entitled *Neelakshi:The Quest for Amrit*.

Interview with Ashok Rajagopalan Sep 7 2013. 5.47 pm by

Dr.G.Mahendranath:

Mahendranath: Sir, please share with us your thoughts regarding stories for children.
Ashok Rajagopalan: A book should understand children - how a child who is born in rural atmosphere communicates, and should communicate accordingly. I see myself as a child in a rural area long ago. I am the subject at hand, the child, when I write. Children are quick learners. Society influences them quickly. The environment is important now and for the future. If we talk to a child, children listen and learn what they are capable of. Most publishers are aware of this. Even in the olden days, we had fables.
Mahendranath: Your experiences as a writer?
Ashok Rajagopalan: I can only imagine my reader. When I draw also, I imagine a child. When I tell stories or interact, I can see whether it reached. Adults refrain from criticising due to politeness but the child directly tells us. We get honest feedback. I relate in different ways to children. I see them as myself as a child. Most successful writers or illustrators retain remembrance of their childhood. For example, drawing with crayons. Because a writer or illustrator for children retains a bit of childhood in him, he cannot look a dignified, older person. He has to be in touch with children. I select something of the child which still exists in me and the childhood of today when I write. Sometimes I feel like a parent. But the best thing for me to do is to adopt the attitude of a friendly tone of voice. A patronizing, older, advising tone in a book sounds like a moral instruction story and is boring. A writer should be a friend who shares – a book should be a friend's talk.
Mahendranath: Can stories make children understand the environment and environmental issues?
Ashok Rajagopalan: Regarding the environment-can't directly advice them. Write a good story and somehow the message comes into it. In the old days there was no disobedience. The child was

unquestioning. In the olden days the authors told stories with morals. Now, we have to entertain children. Tell the message in the form of fiction, subtly weaving in what you wish to convey. Parents used to tell stories to their children and help entertain and educate them. One should lead by example. The sense of discrimination grows gradually in the child. He learns to do good things by following examples. Writers and publishers know this. Parents now feel it is good to ask questions. The child is encouraged to speak out. Democracy has reached children. Children are always curious. They should be encouraged to ask questions. We stop asking questions because we feel insecure. It is our job to answer questions. One question can lead to another. For example, you might tell a story about a parrot called "My parrot." The child can ask: "What is a parrot?" "What do parrots eat?" Kids should open up and learn. The child is sometimes very literal. The child requires a direct answer. About answering a child honestly, if the child asks, "Where doest the sun go?" one can explain about the earth, the sun, the solar system. Or one can say, "The sun sleeps in the sea." Does the child require so much knowledge? What can he listen to? The earth is round, not flat, not round, it is pear shaped? Children might actually a story about "How the monkey got its tail," and "Why the crow is black?" Some people don't like myth. But they help in the development of the imagination.

Mahendranath: What is your opinion about ecological values in Indian children's literature?

Ashok Rajagopalan: Children in English medium schools are not exposed to Indian books. They mainly read Enid Blyton. Unless they read regional languages. Even those books are few in number. Once, I prepared books for a world-wide children's organisation. *Lion Adventure. African Adventure.* Give facts about what the lion is. I used to collect the facts. Children like animals. I don't know about real of nature. But these method works. Books add to knowledge. Children always want to learn. Nature is a thing to learn. This knowledge should be in the form of indirect imparting-fiction and not as direct lessons. Tamil. There are books that I illustrated for the World Vision Project. That organisation had camps for children named Kurunji, Marudham and so on, kinds of geographical divisions of the land in the Tamil literary tradition. I did Kurunji, about the hilly regions. There were stories that directly talked about the environment. Some were indirect. The whole theme was about the environment. *Kaani nilam vendum* (I want a small plot of land) – that was the poet Bharathiar's vision. He wanted 10-12 coconut trees, a hut and a cow in order to attain perfect happiness.

Mahenndranath: What do you perceive is the role of the author and illustrator in conveying ecological messages?

Ashok Rajagopalan: If you want to tell the child, "Do not cut trees for fuel. Use dead wood. A woodcutter who goes to the forest but does not cut trees," you can tell it in the form of a story. King who wanted to build a palace in the forest. What happened, see... Illustrators believe in instilling these values in the child. Successful writers and illustrators should be good communicators. We should ask children their feelings and opinions. Stories should give pleasure and knowledge. But we must tell values, too, through stories so that they will reach the child. Children are fertile soil. They are the future. These efforts will have a lasting effect. They will remain and will become part of them. It is our job to give the recipient of your communication pleasure.

Mahendranath: Can the artist and the writer share a symbiotic relationship?

Ashok Rajagopalan: In nature, there is symbiosis. The relationship between the buffalo and the insects is mutually beneficial. The relationship between the author and the illustrator is not symbiotic. It is essential. Both text and picture are needed. It is like two parts of a message; one cannot be separated from the other. In picture books, pictures and texts are of equal value. Pictures also communicate. Child actually spends times a lot of time looking at the pictures. The text is almost a caption for a picture. The child may not understand the text, but can understand the story from the picture. One co-exists with the other. In an ideal situation, pictures and texts are as equal in value. I have no argument with that. A picture takes up some space. A picture also communicates. "This is how a house made of straw looks like."

Mahendranath: It must be easy to write picture books. Sometimes they have only one line on a page.
Ashok Rajagopalan: One line? Difficult to write that one line. Examples "He is also a naturalist.'" Kalashot is a national park." Shows a girl embracing the front of an elephant. Illustrations help. But the author should also consider the pictures and co-ordinate the text with the pictures.
Mahendranath: What is your favourite method of illustration?
Ashok Rajagopalan: Using oil pastels. You know what they are?
Mahendranath: Yes, Sir. I draw with them, too.
Ashok Rajagopalan: Oh! That's great! Very happy and surprising to know you are an artist.
Mahendranath: Sir! Only as a very small hobby.
Mahendranath: Please tell me about your work in the picture book, *The Black Panther*.
Ashok Rajagopalan: The Black Panther? It was done using a dry brush. That automatically gives emotion.
Mahendranath: Do you meet the authors you illustrate for?
Ashok Rajagopalan: Later on! There was a programme conducted by the British Council. A paper was presented by Ranjit Lal. We were talking about illustrations. Met for the first time, though I had illustrated his books. He said that the publishers showed him its cover afterwards.
Mahendranath: About illustrators and nature?
Ashok Rajagopalan: A really good picture helps the child understand the natural environment and start to love it. It sticks in his mind.
Mahendranath: Do you, as an artist, have a love for nature?
Ashok Rajagopalan: Love for nature? Basically, I think. When we go on an annual family outing, no museum. Spend some time with nature, trees, grass, a kind of silence. I live in Korattur, which is a suburb of Chennai. I don't want to live in a city without trees. Most illustrators artists have love of nature.
Mahendranath: Do you use traditional motifs and art forms?
Ashok Rajagopalan: Traditional art? I would love to, when I can. Nobody has asked this before. Must think. Indian traditional art. Harry Potter was a big success. Magical worlds. They have a

traditions. What I draw is not urban, contemporary. There are some traditional elements in all my books. Tulika [publisher] likes traditional style. This world is a very funny world. Tradition means not to question. That is a bad thing. Dowry, sati are attacked.

Mahendranath: What is your relationship to the text?

Ashok Rajagopalan: The text is important. An artist should be impartial. If the story is about old kingdoms, princes, kings, the illustrations should be appropriate. They should be a visual reflection of what is in the text.

Mahendranath: Are your stories eco-friendly?

Ashok Rajagopalan: Ecofriendly? It is good thing that stories are eco-friendly. This is an age of political correctness. My publishers want to be aware of being politically correct. Tulika-they really care. But other publishers, can't say. You see, they are forced to assume an "eagerness" attitude in their stories You cannot afford to have anyone cutting trees. They have to reflect eco-friendly behaviour.

Mahendranath: What is your contribution to children's literature?

Ashok Rajagopalan: I didn't think about this. I kept on doing my work. J.K.Rowling initiated a revival of interest in children's stories. Her contribution to children's books is great. She gave it status as far as an individual can. Many children are reading big fat books in the age of television and the Internet. My eldest son is 25 years. He started reading J.K.Rowling when he was young. He hadn't read any book before.

Mahendranath: Have you received encouragement from your publishers?

Ashok Rajagopalan: No encouragement. It is this respect, Tulika is the best one. A comment- it is like a sincere political party- there are principles behind the party, as in olden days. Even the publishing house is a commercial organisation. In culture, environment, everything is equal - "One World for All." That is their concept.

Mahendranath: Are your portrayals of animals realistic?

Ashok Rajagopalan: I draw elephants as in *Gajapathi Kulapathi* and not that is not very realistic. An illustration depends upon its text. *The Black Panther* is a realistic book. "Kalia the Crow" unrealistic. But even if you portray it in an unrealistic way, they love the animal. More important how animals are treated. How a nation treats its animals

Mahendranath: Do you have any personal experiences to share about animals?

Ashok Rajagoalan: Two incidents. One is about a stray dog, a small one, which we had as a pet. My father worked in our fields. He returned by scooter in the evening around 4.30. One day he forgot to close the front gate. The dog ran out. My father chased it everywhere. It didn't come back. Mother banged its dish. The dog returned immediately because it thought that dinner-time had come. My wife comes from a cat family. I come from a dog family. Once, our cat climbed a tree and could not come down. It was on a fragile branch. It hung on for dear life. I tried all sorts of things. Sack and long stick used for cutting down branches. Then my wife brought the cat's plate as she does when it is time for lunch. I thought that my wife was crazy. But the cat came down, forgetting the danger.

Mahendranath: For how long have you been illustrating children's books?

Ashok Rajagopalan: Have been writing since 2006 – for more than 6 years now. Have been illustrating for several years before that. Chandamama's magazine for children, Tulika, a lot of other publishers and publishing projects. I gave up my career as an engineer to take up my hobby as a full-time artist.

Mahendranath: Thank you for the valuable inputs, Sir!

Ashok Rajagopalan: It's my pleasure!

MAYA RAMASWAMY

Maya Ramaswamy is one of most respected illustrators of children's books in India. She is specially concerned about conservation and runs an NGO called Artists for Conservation. She has been extensively praised for her fidelity to reality in her pictures. Her works , mainly for Pratham Books and Katha include *A King Cobra's Summer* (2011) *Walk the Grasslands with Takuri* (2010) *Nono the Snow Leopard*.

It is believed that ecological values can be imparted through fiction. Illustrators play a vital role in the child's love and understanding of nature. Could you, as an artist, comment on this?

Illustration is very interesting to children because of the human energy visible through the illustrator's efforts. Hand - work captures the imagination in a very vital sense. So yes, Illustration is a creative medium to bring attention to ecological values.
In picture books and also in all books with pictures, the author and the artist share a symbiotic relationship. From your personal experience as an artist, could you recall some incidents to validate this?
Nature automatically creates the common working ground. A shared passion for nature is needed.
I am sure that you must have a real passion for the natural environment to portray it in an effective manner. Do you love

nature?

Passion is a basic requirement for excellence in any field.
Do you have any personal experiences about the natural environment that you would like to share with us?
Do you use traditional art motifs and other stylistic designs?
No. There is not enough realistic representation of nature in India. I believe relying on traditional styles/motifs would detract from the effectiveness of my work at this stage.

Illustration involves considerable research. Please comment.

Yes, only a lifelong commitment to research, learning and observation can produce good illustration.
How do you work with your authors to give graphical representations to their thoughts?
A common understanding of the subject is required.

What is your own unique contribution to children's books? ----------

What more can be done to represent ecology and the natural environment in children's fiction in India?
Conservation of natural landscapes is vital. Children need to grow up with nature to be complete. No amount of long-term representation of nature in fiction or illustration will help, if our landscapes are sold off for short-term gain to Global Industrial Markets.
We cannot eat cars and televisions. Gold jewelry cannot replace safe, sustainable, fresh water. We need to get our priorities right as a nation.
Please share with us any other thought/comment/suggestion. -----

PRIYA KURIYAN

Priya is an animation film designer who lives and works in New Delhi. She illustrates for children's books and magazines. Priya Kurian is known for her colourful and imaginative illustrations. She has illustrated books for Pratham Publishers, Tulika and Scholastic India among others. She is one of the best- loved children's illustrators today. Her works include *I'm So Sleepy*, *Snoring Shanmugam*, *Colour-Colour Kamini*, *Mallipoo, Where are You?* and *Yes, Hutoxi*.

It is believed that ecological values can be imparted through fiction. Illustrators play a vital role in the child's love and understanding of nature. Could you, as an artist, comment on this?
Illustrations are especially important in kids' books as a children's book would perhaps be a child's first conscious interaction with something artistic and creative. They encourage children's aesthetic appreciation of art and beauty and there is perhaps no better way to introduce aesthetics to a child than to introduce him or her to the natural aesthetics of our environment. Illustrations in picture books also persuade children to read and interact with text thus improving their

vocabulary and also looking for hidden meanings in words. In fact, when kids read picture books that have very little text, they use their heightened imagination to create alternate plots and settings. So, I feel that if picture books have content that talks about nature and has illustrations of the natural environment. Children will definitely be drawn to think about the environment and be interested in it from an early age. Children often associate pictures with their own life experiences. For example ,Once a kid sees a living breathing ,talking tree in a picture book , he would probably empathize more with all the trees that he sees because of the connect he has now made with the picture book tree. In today's day and age where a lot of children live in gated colonies and flats, the interaction with natural environments has reduced considerably making it doubly important for picture books to include nature in their illustrations. However, having said that I would not claim that only by reading picture books can a child connect with the environment. There has to be a conscious role on the part of the parent to encourage the child to go out in the real world and connect with nature .

In picture books and also in all books with pictures, the author and the artist share a symbiotic relationship. From your personal experience as an artist, could you recall some incidents to validate this?
Yes, there are many times when the process of making a book is a symbiotic relationship. The writer and the illustrator bring different talents to the table and often it becomes a learning process for both the writer and the illustrator. The best books come out of good collaborations.
To cite an example, A writer I collaborate with very regularly and I were working on a comic series for 'Brainwave' a science magazine published by Amar Chitra Katha . The comic series was based on various environmental issues and it was set in a world inhabited by the animals of a swamp. During the process of ideation and brainstorming, I was introduced to so many natural phenomena that I didn't know of earlier. In return, I

helped visualize these phenomena and put into images what the writer had in mind. To see their ideas visualized on paper, I hope, gives the writers thought process a boost and even more inspiration to further the series and see more possibilities for other stories.

I am sure that you must have a real passion for the natural environment to portray it in an effective manner. Do you love nature?
I live in Delhi. So, it is difficult to really enjoy a very natural environment on a day to day basis in an urban sprawl. However even Delhi does has its parks and other spaces where one can go and enjoy nature. There are lots of scenic places that one can go to if one tries to travel out of Delhi and I try doing that as often as possible. Also, I would think that I am an environmentally conscious person. I don't think I buy more things than necessary, use public transport whenever I can, segregate waste and have recently moved to buying organic food and trying to do my bit for the environment ☺

Do you use traditional art motifs and other stylistic designs?
I think I'm very inspired by Indian miniature painting and folk art like madhubani, gond etc. I find that my colour palette is a lot like those used in these art forms. Also, nature plays an important role miniatures and folk art too. I love the way they draw trees and flowers. They might not be realistic, but capture the essence of the plant.

Illustration involves considerable research. Please comment.
Yes, it does. Especially when you are making illustrations for kids. The illustrations have to be really accurate in their depiction of things. For example, if the story is set in a certain place, it is important that the illustration you make, represent the people and the environment of the region accurately. One has to understand subtle intricacies of the place that make the characters believable and detailed. For example, if the story is about a baby elephant in India, one will have to look at pictures of elephants to understand what makes an elephant Indian (Its ears) and what is unique about a baby elephant

(Hair poking out of its forehead maybe?) Also what is the environment the elephant lives in? What are the plants that grow there, and so on.

How do you work with your authors to give graphical representations to their thoughts?
I usually read the story a couple of times, a lot of times it is the publisher who acts as a bridge between me and the author. I verbally bounce off some ideas as to how one can treat the story and then do rough pencil sketches to show them. After the first conversation about the book, it's mostly by continuously showing stuff to the author /publisher that the rest of the book is conceived. Once the sketches are approved, I colour one page in order to see what kind of treatment would work best for the book. Once I get an approval on that , I go ahead and colour the book .

What more can be done to represent ecology and the natural environment in children's fiction in India?
I remember reading an article in the New York times a year back, lamenting the slow disappearance of nature in picture books . (I tried googling it again and here it is http://parenting.blogs.nytimes.com/2012/02/29/childrens-books-lose-touch-with-nature/?_r=0) I remember thinking about this at the time and comparing it with Indian children's picture books and what struck me was that the four Indian publishers that made picture books in India , (Tara books , Tulika books, Karadi tales and Katha) definitely had a really good collection of books that directly or indirectly spoke about nature in some way or the other. In fact the last book I did with Tulika called 'When Ali Became Bajrangbali is all about an urban monkey who saves a tree that is home to a number of urban animals (like pigeons, parrots , squirrels and bees) from being cut . The first series of 5 books I did for Tulika called the 'Baby Bahadur series ' is all about a group of animals living together in a forest . Tara books' 'Waterlife' is an exquisite picture book about underwater animals .In that

sense ,I think publishers in India are doing a great job with the amount of space they are giving to the environment . I think what is important is not to make books that are pedagogic when it comes to the environment, but write great stories that make an impression with kids and make them understand how closely connected every organism in the world we live in is and how important the actions of human beings are to making this world a better place to live in.

VANDANA BIST

Vandana Bist has a degree in Fine Arts from the Delhi College of Art and has specialised in illustration. In 1988, she was awarded the encouragement prize in the Children's Picture Book Competition organised by the Noma Concours Foundation, Japan. Her works have been exhibited in Japan and Bratislava. Since 1986, her writings and drawings have been published in various children's magazines and books. Her first book is A Ticket to Home and Other Stories, a collection for children (HarperCollins, 1994). "Surangini" is very popular among children.

It is believed that ecological values can be imparted through fiction. Illustrators play a vital role in the child's love and understanding of nature. Could you, as an artist, comment on this?
An artist creates best when she/he responds to her/his environment. And nature is such an important part of the environment.

In picture books and also in all books with pictures, the author and the artist share a symbiotic relationship. From your personal experience as an artist, could you recall some incidents to validate this?
As an illustrator and a fine artist, I have almost always integrated nature in my works .Some of my works in fine art have represented and translated nature in various degrees of simplicity and complexity.

In my illustrations for children's picture books, some or the other element or elements have consciously or unconsciously found their way into the picture frames.

I am sure that you must have a real passion for the natural environment to portray it in an effective manner. Do you love nature?
I have on many occasions while illustrating a book, sat down with the author and thrashed out in detail the elements of the picture. Nature has often been the topic of our discussions.

From plants in pots and water in pitchers to tropical rain forests and the mighty oceans-all has been grist to my mill.

My works are sure evidence that nature in all its glory and fury and in all its splendor and ordinariness is an integral part of my thoughts and expression.

Do you have any personal experiences about the natural environment that you would like to share with us?
Personal experiences with the natural environment
I think I'm one those blessed persons who had a real green and carefree childhood, spent in the lap of nature. Ever since I can

remember, I've been on close terms with trees,wild gardens,flowers,birds,the beautiful butterflies and the wicked wasps and bees, short tempered mountain rivers and placid lake like rivers in the cities…the list is endless.

Few things are more frightening than a roaring summer storm,more exhilarating than the first shower after a scorching summer, and more peaceful than sitting under an ancient banyan tree,listening to the screeching parakeets and chattering squirrels.

I have found immense peace after venting out my saddest and most depressive feelings to a cluster of trees. I have personally apologized to my potted plants for being careless with them at times and been rewarded with extra brilliant blooms thereafter. It is my firm belief that dogs, cats and pigeons have a way of figuring out your mood and with the help of likeminded people discovered that a garbage dump can be transformed into a beautiful green park.

Do you use traditional art motifs and other stylistic designs?
Use of traditional motifs and designs
Art and culture of all civilizations has used motifs and designs,particularly inspired by nature, at some point or the other.
As an illustrator, I have borrowed generously from varied cultures, as and when the stories required.

Illustration involves considerable research. Please comment.
Research
Research is definitely important if the story being illustrated so requires.
One picture book I worked on had the story located in a land similar to Tibet. A great deal of research went into this work for the pictures to look authentic,particularly the look of the dresses and the buildings.

What is your own unique contribution to children's books?
My contribution
I feel it would be more appropriate if my readers answered this. For myself as a creator of children's picture books, I can for sure say its been and is, a rather fulfilling and gratifying experience.

How do you work with your authors to give graphical representations to their thoughts?

Efforts at representing ecology

Children's fiction as a whole needs to be aggressively addressed in our country. There is a huge paucity of interesting, fun stories for the little and young readers. Fiction for them is largely still stuck at the preachy, holier than thou stage. Having said that, I would admit that there is a conscious change that authors and illustrators of children's books are trying to bring in.

Ecological awareness can only be brought about in children when stories weave this in with an interesting and non- didactic approach.

What more can be done to represent ecology and the natural environment in children's fiction in India?

Please share with us any other thought/comment/suggestion.

I will at the end advise my young friends who wish to pursue Illustration as a career...

If childhood is the least complex of life's phases, writing and illustrating good books for children is the most difficult work ever.

JANUKA DESHPANDE

Junuka Deshpande is a filmmaker, visual artist and photographer who studied communication design at NID, Ahmedabad. She teaches art and is especially concerned about nature and tribal life, which she has studied first-hand as a scholar in Maharashtra. Her use of stylistic devices is imaginative and evocative. She is an author who makes use of illustration, as is seen in her masterpiece, Night, published by Tulika Books.

SR: Do you think children's book should be eco-friendly?
JD: Even the paper that is used to print books should be eco-friendly. Technology can figure out cheaper ways to produce paper.
SR: Illustration, I feel, is very important in children's literature. What do you feel about it?
JD: Before we learn to read or talk, we learn to see. So, seeing is very important. Picture is something that you look at. That creates your perception, your opinion about things. Before children see a tree, they see a picture of the tree. There is an immediate association in the brain. Next time they see something, they will connect with the book. So it is very important that the book has the best art works possible. Not only in terms of the content, but also form. Like..uh..form that is based on famous art or folk things. So it has a dual dimension about it. In my books I usually try to maintain that.
SR: If it is too stylized, won't it be too difficult for the children?
JD: You will be surprised that children understand the abstract better than adults.

SR: Russian books are much stylised. Aren't they?
JD: Yah, even though the stories are very abstract. You know... very heavy and emotionally very evocative kind of stories. Children can understand because they have very perceptive mind. The mind is very fresh.
SR: So, we shouldn't underestimate children.
JD: Yes. We shouldn't look at them as "Ok. I am doing children's literature". I can be realistic. I was taking a story telling session in one of the libraries. The children were more perceptive than the parents who were sitting there. I had projected these images on a large screen. The children came out with sounds that are not even mentioned here. They didn't read the text. They were looking at the images and building their own texts. They even named the children on their own.

SR: Wonderful, no?

JD: Yah, wonderful. I think what a book should do to children is to inspire them to come up with their own ideas...inspired by ecology.

SR: So, when the children grow up they will be better citizens.

JD: Yes, better citizens. And next time after the session if the child goes out to the streets, he will immediately connect. "Oh, this is a city...this is a vehicle. In the jungle there are no vehicles...there is silence".

SR: They can at least see the silence in the book. That is the best part of it.

JD: The book should do that instead of explaining every thing. Even fairly tales do a lot of explanation. I don't like *Cindrella* or similar stories. They don't give inspiration to children to think on their own because it is from other world. We should tell stories from our own world. Drawing, as I said, creates perception. Visuals create perception; visuals make an image about every thing in your brain. That is why it is important that you create an authentic image.

SR: Even the mythological cartoons have some funny faces presented in a western way. And, it is the same even with Krishna and the other cartoons.

JD: Yah. Even though the story is Indian, the style is western. So, it doesn't make sense again.

SR: How did you start doing story illustration?

JD: I used to draw pictures even as a small girl. And, I did the illustration for a very important book when I was thirteen. That created a huge impact because it was a sensitive age. I was also reading literature then. That is when the whole interest developed.

SR: Reading makes you imagine a lot.

JD: Yah, I was reading vernacular literature in Marathi. That was good because I got to read a lot of famous works. I could connect with that. So, the drawing automatically became very appropriate because I was so involved.

SR: Were you inspired or influenced by Marathi folk lore?

JD: No, then I was drawing intuitively...whatever came to my mind. I had no idea about the design process. Later on, I went to the design school and learnt how to design a book...how to go about it... and that there are other people who draw. I started looking at them. But before that I was drawing intuitively.

SR: You decided your profession quite early in life?

JD: No, initially I wanted to become a doctor because I was very interested in the human body. But then, I went to NID and liked the place when I went there for the interview. I felt "this is the place. I would meet creative people". It is a different world altogether. I connected a lot with that world.

SR: You must have been very lucky to have met all those people?

JD: Yah, That's right. I was very lucky that I made it to NID.

SR: May be because of your interest...

JD: Yah, may be. After that, I found my passion. I was into making films, drawing, painting and teaching.

SR: Like a multi-sensitive personality? Everything is related...

JD: Right, everything is related.

SR: What is the difference between drawings and movies?

JD: It is a different medium.

SR: Is there a relationship?

JD: One very obvious relation is that we think in visuals.

SR: So, a lot of psychology goes into it?

JD: Yes. A lot of experience also goes into it. If I have to create a character or a story, I should know where that story is coming from. I should have the ability to tell stories through everything around me. So, that is what we do with drawing. Illustrations do the same thing.

SR: Have you ever done a documentary for children or about nature?

JD: No, but I have done a documentary about forest...about the tribal communities in Madhya Pradesh. It is not for children; it is about the problems that the tribal communities are facing. There is a big conflict between the government policies and the tribes who want to conserve the forests. The government is trying to move them out from there. The people don't cut down trees; they only collect the fruits and stuff. People have been conserving forests for ages. The government policies just can't see how people can live inside forests. I would like to tell the stories of conservation.

SR: I think there are picture books for adults also...?
JD: Yah. There are multimedia novels.
SR: What are multimedia novels?
JD: Something that you can read on ipad...you don't need paper...you can save paper.
SR: Still, we can't avoid using paper.
JD: Recently I read in the newspaper that we can make paper out of elephant dung.
SR: Do you have a passion for the national environment?
JD: Yes, I do.
SR: Have you had any personal experience in the forest?
JD: I had to go to forests in Madhya Pradesh and Gujarat for my documentary.
SR: Can you remember anything special?
JD: I got back a lot in terms of experience. I observed and learnt how people live in sync with nature.
SR: Anything unusual? Anything unexpected?
JD: Silences ... We become more aware when we are in the forest. We may not be doing anything, but at the same time we do things on a different level.
SR: Like the Rishis going to mountains?
JD: Yah. We all lead fast lives. In urban life we feel that we are doing a lot. We are always in a rush. We don't get time to think. Life is mechanised.
SR: For creative people if there is no time to think, it is very sad.
JD: Right. My work does help me to be with nature at times, but what about the others who do not have the time to observe...to feel...to understand. Somewhere we are forgetting the beauty of nature.
SR: We are missing something very precious.
SR: Moving on, do you use traditional motifs?
JD: I don't use them directly, but yes I am inspired by them.

SR: I think traditional colours are very attractive.
JD: Yes.

SR: Why is it so?
JD: I think our people have thought about it. In our psyche nature is very strong. People can easily associate with colours of nature. Just like *Rangoli*. It is symbolic.
SR: Can you tell something about the symbols? Actually, I have done something on symbolism for my PhD thesis.
JD: I have not studied it, but I know that it represents. Many people have worked on the "tree of life".
SR: In literature too we have that.
JD: To me, experience comes first. Then I look for what other people have done. Sometimes I am very spontaneous. Then I draw the way I think. Sometimes I read books from other styles. Sometimes it is poetry or even story. So different things can inspire you. So when you are going about illustration you should go through all this.
SR: Which character do you take maximum interest in The Mahabharata as far as illustration is concerned?
JD: Bheeshma. There is a story about the making of Bheeshma. I find it very fascinating.
SR: Sad character right?
JD: Yah. The interesting part is that when I got the work I was not a lover of mythology. I wasn't really interested in mythology. Then I read the story and got interested. Sometimes that happens. The projects can get you interested in things you are generally not interested.
SR: Surely, you would have watched the serials.
JD: Yah, but all that did not interest me…the magic…the war. It really did not interest me. Then when I read the story I became interested. I don't try to show exactly what the story says. I put my bits into it and then I show it.
SR: Do you frequently communicate with the authors?
JD: Yah, all the time.
SR: Usually the interaction is with the publisher…

JD: No, I always communicate with the authors so that I can get instant feedback. Sometimes we differ in perspectives. The authors will have something else.

SR: Since you are an author you will understand both the sides.

JD: Yah. And, that is a part of the job. It is also very enriching. You learn a lot from each other in the process and learn how other people think.

SR: What is your unique contribution to children's books?

JD: Actually, I haven't done that much for children. But I really want to do.

SR: What more can be done to represent ecology and the environment in children's fiction?

JD: I think we should work on the originality of our drawings and therefore pay attention to authentic representation of our own environment.

SR: You told me that Krishna looks like Tom n Jerry...

JD: Yah. We should pay attention. As illustrators, our drawings should talk about our environment. Even if you are telling a story about a city there should be an element of our environment because it represents an important part of us. Our stories should consciously have these elements. As illustrators, we should see how we can bring in these elements.

SR: Would you like to share anything else on children's fiction?

JD: I think that's it.

SR: As an author and illustrator, let me ask you something. Mostly we have a lot of non-fiction and prescribed text books for ecology. Do you think fiction plays a good role in inculcating values?

JD: Yah, if it is friendly enough. Actually, I am not an author as such. In fact I drew this book first before I sent her the concept. I sent her six illustrations. So I draw my stories. I don't write in words. I don't know how text actually works. I know how visuals work.

SR: But you are planning to come up with books?

JD: Yah, but it will be pictorial. Words don't come to me naturally.

SR: So you are a visual thinker.

JD: I think so. Even if I am thinking of an idea I share with you, I think in visuals.
SR: Like a dancer.
JD: Yah, may be. That's my medium. I don't know how text works. I haven't studied it. I am not experienced in that area.
SR: Do you read children's books?
JD: Yah, I do.
SR: So do you have anything to say about children's books?
JD: In the sense?
SR: Anything that should be done...which has not been done so far.
JD: Yah, that's what I am saying. We should tell more stories in Indian context...every day life stories...might interest children. I think we should make more books like that so that children become more sensitive towards their environment.

SR: What do say about the unrealistic portrayal of animals?
JD: Which books are you talking about?
SR: There are books in which animals have to talk...and they can not be portrayed realistically.
JD: OK. It depends on what the message of the book is....What the objective of the book is...like some of them are very very artistic books...like the animals in this book are not realistic.
SR: They appear to be very real.
JD: No, they are not realistic at all. But yet they convey a message. So it all depends on the message actually. What kind of book it is. A lot of things go into it. Some times our clients want realistic portrayal...especially in text books.
SR: Of course.
JD: You have to draw exactly like real life.
SR: Thank you so much.

What the Editors and Publishers Have to Say

Himanshi Sharma, TERI Books, New Delhi

TERI, The Energy and Resources Institute, based in New Delhi, was formally established in 1974 with the purpose of tackling and dealing with the immense and acute problems that mankind is likely to face within in the years ahead. Its growth-rate has been tremendous and its presence is now international. TERI has a formidable array of publications to offer. The aim of its children's imprint, Terrapin, is to create awareness about environmental issues among young people. It has a range of fiction and non-fiction to offer.
QUESTIONS TO PUBLISHERS-Himansi Sharma, Editor, TERI Books
How is the publishing scenario with regard to books for children and young adults in India today? –
 I believe this industry hasn't still established completely, and there are no formal training programs or courses pertaining to this field. One can gauge the situation only by realizing that there are only a handful of exclusive children's bookstores in a place like Delhi.

Environmental science is part of the curriculum of most schools and colleges. Still, light reading in the form of fiction helps inculcate values. Do you agree?
Yes, certainly, it does, as it makes the content interesting.
Do you think ecological wisdom can be imparted through fiction? Please state your opinion.. **Yes. TERI is doing that by means of its books.**
Does your publishing house give importance to stories projecting ecological value – for example, depicting eco-friendly behavior, condemning environmentally unhealthy practices, the importance of biodiversity, environmental pollution and other problems, dilemmas and solutions, etc.? If yes, please specify
.Yes, of course. Our titles bring out the message of environment, healthy living, and sustainable development by means of stories or non-fiction titles.
Love of nature automatically creates awareness about the need for its conservation. Do the stories in your books have nature as a background? –
Yes, of course. Please refer to our online bookstore.
Are animals realistically and sensibly portrayed?
Yes. Always. We don't wish to convey the wrong message to young learners.
Is the traditional way of life, especially the lives of traditional people depicted in a positive manner?
Yes
Do you have any special personal relationship with the natural environment?
Yes
Illustrations are vital to children's books. How do you make use of illustrations to enhance the implicit message of your books?
Illustrations make books speak, in a way, and help children relate with them better.
Are your books eco-friendly? For example, do you use recycled paper?
Yes, we use 100% recycled paper. What's the point of preaching something that we can't practice.

Do you follow innovative practices in design to enhance you books? (for example, using traditional stylistic designs)
Yes

What is your personal relationship with the natural environment? Do you follow eco-friendly practices in real life?
Yes, working in my present organization, which works for sustainable development, has brought a positive change in my life. I have learnt to be more responsible and I do not waste resources now.

As a publisher, do you feel that ecology and the natural environment have found adequate and favourable representation in fiction for children and young adults in India?
Yes. But it still needs to go a long way.

Can you further enlighten us/ give suggestions/comments/further experiences?
All that I can suggest is that you buy our books and get first-hand experience.

Questions to YA Publishers

The youth of today can play a crucial role in averting ecological disaster.
Yes

What can publishers do to remind youth of their responsibilities regarding the environment?
Publish books that sensitize youth about these issues.

Can you share with us any personal experience regarding nature?
Research has proved that people are happiest when in the vicinity of nature. And I have experienced this too, whenever I go out of Delhi and experience the life beyond Metro cities.

TARA BOOKS

Tara Books is a unique Chennai-based publishing house that produces picture books for both children and adults. The books are printed on handmade paper, specially designed and printed using the silkscreen method. The publishing house takes special pride in planting trees to replace the paper used. Tara has won a considerable number of awards.

QUESTIONS TO PUBLISHERS
How is the publishing scenario with regard to books for children and young adults in India today?
There are a wealth of publishing houses bringing out titles in both English and regional languages.
Environmental science is part of the curriculum of most schools and colleges. Still, light reading in the form of fiction helps inculcate values. Do you agree?
Yes. Supplementing the school curriculum with engaging reading material (both fiction and non-fiction) has always been important in bringing topics to life for both children and adults.

Do you think ecological wisdom can be imparted through fiction? Please state your opinion.

Yes, books (both fiction and non-fiction) have the potential to portray powerful narratives. We specialise in picture books, and the folk and tribal artists that we work with have been successful in conveying alternative world-views in the work that we have published. A good example of this would be *The Night Life of Trees* which Publishers Weekly described as: "A glowingly mysterious and charming volume ... This mingling of the mythic, mundane and poetic gives an alluring glimpse into an integrative worldview that's in poignant contrast to the fragmented postmodern world."

Does your publishing house give importance to stories projecting ecological value – for example, depicting eco-friendly behavior, condemning environmentally unhealthy practices, the importance of biodiversity, environmental pollution and other problems, dilemmas and solutions, etc.? If yes, please specify.

Around 30% of our books are made entirely by hand (through the silkscreen printing process) in our Book Craft workshop. We are a labour-intensive press to start with: our handmade print workshop employs over 18 men. We work mostly with handmade paper, procured from paper mills in Tamil Nadu, and this is paper made from grain and vegetable and fruit waste. We try and use non-toxic ink as much as we can though this is not always easy. And we adhere to EU and American standards, as far as the quality of ink, levels of chemical saturation etc. are concerned. The binding is also done by hand (hand-stitched).

We also recycle the misprints created in the silkscreen printing process (sheets that don't pass quality control and test sheets) to create flukebook covers – our one-of-a-kind notebooks.

For the offset printed books (which are printed largely in China and make up the other 70% of our output) we try and source recycled paper as far as possible, for example in our graphic novels *Sita's Ramayana* and *I See the Promised Land*.

Love of nature automatically creates awareness about the need for its conservation. Do the stories in your books have nature as a background?
We work largely with artists from India's rich folk and tribal art traditions. As many of these artists hail from a rural context, nature is a strong and reoccurring theme in many of our books. For example, we have worked extensively with artists from the Gond tribe of central India, who have their roots in a densely forested region. As such the tree looms large in their creative output. Examples of books that we have published would include *The Night Life of Trees* and *Alone in the Forest*.

Are animals realistically and sensibly portrayed?
We work largely with artists from India's rich folk and tribal art traditions: community art traditions. One of the most significant features of community art is that it is representational, but non-realistic, unconcerned with the appearance of things as they are. Perspective, light, proportions, or likeness are unimportant. Community art is figurative or iconic, rendered through lines, colour and decorative elements, each with its own grammar and symbolism. Unlike modern western art which is self conscious in its departure from realism, community art is radical in its understanding of art as artifice. Reality and the imagination are never confused with each other, and always kept separate.

Is the traditional way of life, especially the lives of traditional people depicted in a positive manner?
Tara's ongoing dialogue with the incredibly rich and varied forms of indigenous tribal and folk art in India goes back over a decade. We work with artist from different – and often very remote – communities, bringing their work into the form of a book. These range from children's picture books to collections of art prints.
Our collaborations with these artists take many forms: from nudging them to illustrate new stories, to asking them to tell their own. Most of them are from very poor and marginalised

groups, but the talent, intelligence and imagination that we have encountered is humbling.

We're privileged that in India, unlike in many parts of the world, these artists are our active contemporaries. We hope that our interactions with them retain the essence of what makes each style distinctive, while bringing it into the contemporary publishing discourse.

Our aim is to enable each artist to be an author: the active creator of a book. So these books don't just document a particular art tradition, they are the location from which the form and the artist can speak for themselves. Only by giving a voice – an agency – to those who normally have no access to the book, can we shift the focus from the usual class-bound and homogenous points of view that we are used to

Illustrations are vital to children's books. How do you make use of illustrations to enhance the implicit message of your books?

The visual is absolutely central to all of our books, and we see it as a way to transcend the barriers set up by language, caste and class.

Are your books eco-friendly? For example, do you use recycled paper?

See above

Do you follow innovative practices in design to enhance you books? (for example, using traditional stylistic designs)

Where the art form allows, we silkscreen print by hand. This is the case for around 30% of our books.

As a publisher, do you feel that ecology and the natural environment have found adequate and favourable representation in fiction for children and young adults in India?

It's hard to comment on the work of others, but you may find a recent article that I have attached helpful.

MALA KUMAR, CHILDRENS' AUTHOR AND PUBLISHER OF PRATHAM BOOKS, BANGALORE

QUESTIONS TO PUBLISHERS
How is the publishing scenario with regard to books for children and young adults in India today?
It is looking up. Our readership is so diverse that to reach all children is a challenge. There are so many languages, so many socio-cultural segments, so many different school systems to cater to.
Environmental science is part of the curriculum of most schools and colleges. Still, light reading in the form of fiction helps inculcate values. Do you agree?
Yes.
Do you think ecological wisdom can be imparted through fiction? Please state your opinion.
Definitely. The setting of a story lingers in a reader's mind.
Does your publishing house give importance to stories projecting ecological value – for example, depicting eco-friendly behavior, condemning environmentally unhealthy practices, the importance of biodiversity ,environmental pollution and other problems, dilemmas and solutions, etc.? If yes, please specify.
We are very clear about projecting ecological values. We have books on rivers. We have books on wildlife. *A King Cobra's*

Summer, set in the Western Ghats is about a snake, but the reader is sure to learn a lot about ecology and biodiversity through this book. Similarly, *Muchkund and his Sweet Tooth* is a fictional take on bees and ecology.

Love of nature automatically creates awareness about the need for its conservation. Do the stories in your books have nature as a background?

Many do have this.

Are animals realistically and sensibly portrayed?

In the books for older children, yes. In books for younger children, our lions talk, our hippos jump on the moon, and many other fantastic things do happen.

Yes. We have a series of books *Is the traditional way of life, especially the lives of traditional people depicted in a positive manner?*

woven around families of artisans like weavers, and potters.

Do you have any special personal relationship with the natural environment?

As publishers, we are conscious of environmental best practices. We encourage our volunteers to hold storytelling sessions in parks, under trees etc. We are also working with several environmentalists on various books.

Illustrations are vital to children's books. How do you make use of illustrations to enhance the implicit message of your books?

We ensure we work with illustrators who are environmentally well-informed. Many of our illustrators conduct workshops for children on recyling, art through wste etc.

Are your books eco-friendly? For example, do you use recycled paper?

We have used water-based ink and recycled paper for our book *Cauvery*.

Do you follow innovative practices in design to enhance you books? (for example, using traditional stylistic designs)

Yes. We have books illustrated in many traditional styles.

What is your personal relationship with the natural environment? Do you follow eco-friendly practices in real life?

Yes.

As a publisher, do you feel that ecology and the natural environment have found adequate and favourable representation in fiction for children and young adults in India?
Publishers seem to be doing a good amount, but we need more books that are less preachy and more realistic.
Can you further enlighten us/ give suggestions/comments/further experiences?
We need more books on environment beyond the 'Don't cut trees', save water kind. When children read well-written stories about animals and birds, that are atrractive in presentation, language and style, they will tend to respect nature much more than if the values are pushed down their throats.

Interview with Saraswathy Rajagopalan, Editor, Mango Books, Kochi

Mango is the children's imprint in English brought out by DC Books. They focus on Indian content and stories from different parts of the world.. Enriched with creative designs, brilliant editing and clever use of English language, their books are not just an entertaining read but a visual treat as well. Old Indian classics are presented in a refreshingly new style and bold stories about contemporary India are part of our extensive list. A new line of books focusing on ecology and the environment are the highlights of this enterprising publishing house.

Mrs.Saraswathi: This is out new book which will be released next month- *Vriksha: Original Tree Stories and Tree Facts.* It is a story of a tree with the ecological aspects and the environment by Vinitha Ramchandani. It's just out, not in shops. These are like advance copies.
Me: Is it about the environment? How is the response?
Mrs.Saraswathi: It's going well, good timing. This is another book called *Meera's friends, the Trees* by Jayshree Mishra and Deepika Jain. It sold out. It is a fiction based on the Chipko Movement and it is very sensitive. We are also planning sending to press is also about trees. 'Autobiography of a Tree.' It's written originally in

Bengali by Saroj Mukerjee. Then in Hindi and now it's coming to English, translated by Shobha Tharoor Sreenivasan.

Me: Is it fiction?

Mrs.Saraswathi: It is fiction. It is the story of a tree. Sometimes it is very subtle where again, the tree watching everything- the girl growing up, a soldier getting amputated and also saying that: " Let me note I stand for a long time but I don't stand for ever. "

Me: It reminds us about the Raaji story, "The Tree Speaks."The tree also has some soul. One of the short stories.

Mrs.Saraswathi: That's very similar, I would say. And we have also done one which is now actually sold out. It is a very good one, which is written by Jaishree Mishra and Geetika Jain. It is called *Meera's Friends, the Trees*. It's a fiction based on Chipko Movement, that was very successful. It is actually out of print now. So I can't given you a copy now.

Me; How sad, I like Jaishree Mihsra's works.

Mrs.Saraswathi: Yeah, she wrote for us, and then the other one which we did which was quite similar, was written by Bombay based author, Anita Vachharajani. It is called *Tara Tambe, Forest Friend*. It's not yet out. If you want I can email the cover of the books, if that is any help.

Me: Yes, please.

Mrs.Saraswathi: *Meera's Friends the Trees* did extremely well. Then there is another series which talks about ecology. I don't you you may also be thinking about animals. That's an entire series written by its called Kerala Mystique. Every one of them is actually about animals. Like "Unni's Story." There is an elephant there. "Turtle Tales" is about a girl, a slightly troubled child because she had lost both of her parents and now she finds the cynical relationship with a small turtle.

Me: The title's familiar- "Turtle Tales."

Mrs.Saraswathi: Yeah, it's when Kirthivarman is the king and then you know, finally, she releases the turtle back into the sea and then she makes peace. And then there is one called "Mallika" about a snake. It tells children that the snake is never going to bite you unless you go out of your way to harm it. Then there is one called "When the Mountain Laughed." It's about the boy who is very upset about the dark colour of his skin, so he thinks he is always being discriminated. In the original thing, the boy wants to end his life but we thought it was not the nice thing. While he goes to the mountain it just laughs at him and tells him,, "You really can't do this."

Me: Is it based on a folktale or is it original?

Mrs.Saraswathi: These are all original and then there is another one also. Its about the person all these children call "Pisashu"- he is the one who is so much in tune with nature. It is something unique. The story of someone who loves nature, seen through the eyes of children. One who loves animals and mountains. Actually, in a way that there is so much to learn. So much. It still remains one of the best series we have done. How many people look upon it in the same light is uncertain.

Me: It may be that you love nature because you live in Kerala. You have such good scenery here.

Mrs.Saraswathi (smiling):No, we leave it to the author. We have a process, but we choose the stories that we like. So there are quite a few on the environment. Come Monday, when we send the other one to the press, we want to bundle this up. We must sort it out with Long, Long Ago. The people supply books to schools. They buy quite a few copies from us.

Me: Me: Long, Long Ago, the library?

Mrs.Saraswathi: They are our distributors in Coimbatore.They do take quite a lot of Mango books. They like this book very much. Such a lot of orders. We have quite a lot of orders actually from them, even Japanese folk tales. But these are actually I think, very specific- more this is fact-fiction about all these trees in India. What really is the story behind them, what is the belief. We have actually said that because children cannot believe,in this time and age, "Look, this is how the mango- got its name, why the coconut stands so tall, Indira coming down." But there is it was popular belief and we give all scientific facts of tree -you know, where does grow. So it is going to be launched this month in Bookaroo.

Me: In New Delhi?

Mrs.Saraswathi: Yes. We have for the now stopped this magazine which was a forthnightly and became a monthly magazine in which we used to publish a few pages on the environment and nature.

Me:Oh!

Mrs.Saraswathi:Yes, we are doing it quite a lot because we something we should do.

Me: Fiction is a vehicle for conveying all the textbooks on the environment. I think if you tell the story, to a child, I think all these messages will get through.

Mrs.Saraswathi:Definitely. Definitely. Especially when the book has good illustrations.

Me: So you give a lot of importance to illustrations?

Mrs.Saraswathi:Yes. In fact, illustrations help a lot. It is one of the biggest parts of a book. In fact, they say that children go back to the illustrations. Even if they don't read the story again, they go to the illustrations. And getting the right illustrator of the story. We focus on that.

Me: Do you Priya Kuiryan, who is from Kochi, now based in Delhi?

Mrs.Saraswathi: I know her. She did 'How Hyderabad came to be.' It is a folktale which is actually about nature. Then who is the illustrator. That is important.

Me: Children remember the illustrations more than the text?

Mrs.Saraswathi: They do. Even us, even now. A lot of books which stick in our minds, ones which we even go back to because children's books are so comforting -there is a world that is comforting in many children's books, not all- and then you go back for the illustrations.

Me: Who are your main authors?

Mrs.Saraswathi: Viitha Ramchandan, Nandini Nayar, Anita Vachharajani, Rema Jayaraman, Shobha Tharoor Sreenivasan, Sashi Tharoor's sister, Sheila Dhar, Jaishree Mishra, Geetika Jain.

Me: Do you encourage new authors?

Mrs.Saraswathi: We do. Right now what someone has written to me, is a very interesting story on a spider. In fact, we have a project we are doing right now. I have asked her to give me three weeks time since we have a particular process. We can't make books only about ecology, but many books we have done, especially the original works are about nature.

Me: What about your distribution network? Do you do your distribution directly?

Mrs.Saraswathi:We have a complete setup in Kerala. Malls such as Lulu Mall, then the shops. Distribution is our high point. In fact, our warehouse is just down the road, next to YMCA. As you know, we have a few distributors in other states.

Me:What is your price range? It is within the reach of children?

Mrs.Saraswathi:I think our price range is reasonable. We have books for Rs.95/-. This one about Endangered Animals, has a higher price range, because it is hardbound, with high quality paper. But say, this format, (showing book) is always 95 rupees. Softbound. We experimented with this format (hardbound), because at Rs.245/- the market is a bit low. Now this one, *Story of My Experiments With Truth*, is selling very well. We have *History Fun and Facts*. But then we are sellling at 95/. Some the pricing will be good when the volumes are more. We try to keep it at Rs.60/- when we have 4000 numbers. We are trying to bring out different sorts of books as well.

Me: Do you sell to schools in Coimbatore?

Mrs.Saraswathi: We are not very familiar with schools in Coimbatore. Generally higher end schools, because of the content. Because, you know, we have retellings of Shakespeare. A set for prize distribution will not cost much. The Gandhi book, is of course, doing very well. But this (Endangerd Animals) is equally sophisticated and even if we price this half, whether people will understand its value for children or not has to be seen. But what sells and qualifies for children's books are retellings. Even when we get orders- we have a person who works the entire marketing, Andhra- he says, "Madam, they will take these without a second glance.' (about retellings).

Me: Nobody goes for creativity.

Mrs. Saraswathi: That is very true. That is very true. We take that on an experimental basis. So if you send these book lists to the average bookseller in Chennai, he wants10 copies each of Fairy Tales.

Me: I've seen in the bookshops that they don't have sufficient space for children's books. They have the foreign ones, but no space forIndian books.

Mrs.Saraswathi: Yes, that is true.

Me: Sad.

Mrs.Saraswathi: We are strong because we are somewhat in the middle. We have moderate pricing and very good quality. It is a solid sort of thing and good. We are not catering to a very niche readership. I mean we have projects on which we are working, but the idea is reach out to as many people as possible

Me: Zai Whitaker said that publishers re initially enthusiastic, but later on they do not push the book much.

Mrs.Saraswathi: Who said this?

Me: Zai Whitaker.

Mrs.Sarasathi:The publishing in there, but I don't blame the people for this. You see, there is a very strong publishing house here in DC, Malayala Maampazham, but otherwise people are only publishing in Hindi. So there is a limit to what audience we can reach out to. But still then, there is a lot of publicity, a lot of events, a lot of people are involved. But in India, we are sort of Delhi-centric. It all happens in Delhi.

Me: Do you export?

Mrs. Saraswathi: Yes we do. But we also sell rights. We have sold threrights of our versions of Ramayana, Mahabharatha and Experiments with Truth, and we have a retelling of the Buddha story for which we have sold rights.

Me: I saw on the notice board a photograph of your publishing house receiving an award from a Gulf country.

Mrs. Saraswathi (pleased): That was the Sharjah Book Fair. We got the award for Best International Publishers. DC Books did. Our USP is that we are on the scale of an independent publisher, but you go into a multinational setup. That is happening in DC Books and Mango Books.

Me: Do you have audio books as well?

Mrs.Saraswathi: Yes. In fact, we are closing our project quite literally as we speak. In fact, we have 100 audio books and planning to expand.

Me: How did you fix on the name "Mango Books"?

Mrs.Saraswathi: At first, we were "Thumbi."

Me: That means "beetle"?

Mrs.Saraswathi: Yes. But because it travels a lot and most people started calling it 'thambi' (younger brother), we discussed it and changed it to "Mango."

Me: It's very striking and Indian.

Mrs.Sarasathi: Yes, and it sits in the mind and as a spoken word also, it is nice.

Me: How long have you been publishing as Mango Books?

Mrs.Saraswathi: For 6 years.

Me: I saw your website. It is informative and attractive.

Mrs.Saraswathi: Yes, we have updated it.

Me: can I contact your authors?

Mrs.Sarasathi: You want to speak to Prabha Ram. Please drop a line, and I will send her contact information. And Vinitha is also very open. So is Lavanya Karthik who does the illustrations.

Me: Thank you very much for the wonderful interview!

Mrs.Saraswathi: You are welcome!

SHOBHA VISWANATH – PUBLISHING DIRECTOR AND CO- FOUNDER, KARADI TALES, CHENNAI

Co-founder and Publishing Director of Karadi Tales Company, Shobha Viswanath has been responsible for steering the direction of the publishing house from brilliantly produced audio-books for children to new imprints such as Dreaming Fingers (illustrated books for the visually disabled), Charkha (inspiring audio biographies for young adults), and Chitra (beautifully

Interview with Shobha Viswanath

What made you interested in this area, about the books reflecting nature and ecological questions?

When Karadi Tales began, we primarily focused on bringing out audiobooks based on existing folktales and mythological stories. As we gradually began to widen our publishing list, we wanted to add to our repertoire of books, stories that addressed contemporary and universal themes. We brought out titles such as *The Bookworm* (that addresses bullying) and *Crickematics* (the fear of Maths), and *Dorje's Stripes* and *Dancing Bear* (animal rights and environmental conservation). While *Dancing Bear* was inspired by the stories of The Qalandars - a gypsy tribe that propagated the cruel act of bear-dancing in India – *Dorje's Stripes* was written, keeping in mind the dwindling tiger population in the world. These two books were recommended as part of Young India Books' Leading Reading Schools of India Awards 2015 programme. *The Lizard's Tail* is another Karadi Tales title that is based on nature and science. This is a simple, cyclical story that deals with the concept of tail regeneration in lizards.

One of our recent titles, *Thea's Tree,* a wonderful picturebook by Judith Clay, is set in a futuristic world without trees. This story takes on the alarming message of ecological damage in a hopeful way. This book was listed in The White Ravens 2012 catalogue of notable and remarkable international children's books (the catalogue is published by the Internationale Jugendbibliothek in Munich).

How do illustrations help?

Illustrations in picturebooks are as important as text; the verbal and the visual narratives work together to communicate the story to the reader. *Dorje's Stripes* and *Dancing Bear* have been illustrated by Korean artists, Gwangjo and Jung-a Park, and they feature sensitive illustrations in watercolour to reflect the nature of the themes that the stories address. The beautiful illustrations in *Thea's Tree,* by the author herself, create the stark contrast between a world without trees and a world with trees through the use of cold and warm colors. The illustrations enhance the poignancy of the stories and convey, by themselves, the message of ecological responsibility.

Why is fiction important in installing Eco values?

Stories are the best way to communicate any message to children, aren't they? (Preachy, boring ones don't count though.)

Have you plans for conducting activities for children/ any other future plans?

We have been working on a series titled 'Kavi the Xplorer', which contains stories about a smart, little boy who is curious about nature; caterpillars and strange birds to be more specific. We are also commissioning more stories that deal with environmental issues.

Any suggestions as a publisher, editor, author and teacher?

It would be encouraging to see authors, editors and publishers work together to bring out more non-didactic books focusing on issues addressing the environment. We have enough textbook material dealing with these topics; we require entertaining books for children that implicitly convey the message of environmental awareness.

Dr. MINI KRISHNAN

Dr. Mini Krishnan is Literary Translations Editor at Oxford Universitypress,Chennai.She was formerly Branch Editor,Macmillan India.She initited the *Living in Harmony* series for children.

QUESTIONS TO PUBLISHERS

How is the publishing scenario with regard to books for children and young adults in India today?
Extremely uneven. Children are not treated with much respect and all the publishing is geared to attracting the attention of parents. Barring a few publishers in English no attention is paid to the child's mental growth or vocabulary or language attainment

Environmental science is part of the curriculum of most schools and colleges. Still, light reading in the form of fiction helps inculcate values. Do you agree?
Of course. Many epic battles and resistances are about protection of Bhoomi mata and it would be wrong to not encourage children to identify with their environment. Several myths also show mountains,rivers and trees to be alive and participating in human lives

Do you think ecological wisdom can be imparted through fiction? Please state your opinion.

Anything can be successfully carried through in fiction: love of land, of parents, of tradition, and a healthy sense of earth ethics surely

Does your publishing house give importance to stories projecting ecological value – for example, depicting eco-friendly behavior, condemning environmentally unhealthy practices, the importance of biodiversity, environmental pollution and other problems, dilemmas and solutions, etc.? If yes, please specify.

You can study the textbooks in environment studies and peace studies that Oxford University Press has published. We have carried many Peace Posters in a series Ive edited called Living in Harmony. Please take a look at the centre page spreads ...they are about environment and spiritualizing Nature

Love of nature automatically creates awareness about the need for its conservation. Do the stories in your books have nature as a background?

Please do your own research. Specifically the set of books called Living in Harmony for classes 1-2-3-4-5-6-7-8 published by Oxford University Press

Are animals realistically and sensibly portrayed?

Very sympathetically, I do not know about realism

Is the traditional way of life, especially the lives of traditional people depicted in a positive manner?

Yes we have whole lessons on the tribal way of life and are in the process of developing an art page all of which are from traditional folk arts of India

Do you have any special personal relationship with the natural environment?

If you mean do I spend time alone in an isolated spot—no. But if animals come into this equation, my answer is yes, I support Green Earth, I'm a regular donor to Blue Cross and the Indian Institute of Animal Welfare and have always had dogs at home who are part of the family

Illustrations are vital to children's books. How do you make use of illustrations to enhance the implicit message of your books?

This is usually done by the designer not the editor but I did design the Peace Pages of the OUP Value Education series as Ive already outlined

Are your books eco-friendly? For example, do you use recycled paper?

No, recycled paper is too expensive to use in textbooks the burden of which has then to be borne by the student

Do you follow innovative practices in design to enhance you books? (for example, using traditional stylistic designs)

Not especially because the student market does not like surprises. Teachers are the last to change their tastes and preferences

What is your personal relationship with the natural environment? Do you follow eco-friendly practices in real life?

Yes I do but they are too tedious to narrate here and one cannot always carry out one's personal preferences in a corporate situation

As a publisher, do you feel that ecology and the natural environment have found adequate and favourable representation in fiction for children and young adults in India?

No but we have come a long,long way. When I was a child and Im talking about 50 years ago the very word was missing in the minds of the public and the vocabulary of the popular imagination.Remember that *Silent Spring* was published only in 1962.

Can you further enlighten us/ give suggestions/comments/further experiences?

I feel that every newspaper in all the languages of India should have a Nature for Children page to which students are encouraged to contribute. Unless a certain ownership and responsibility for the environment is built the care of the Earth will become someone else's duty and not mine.

INTERVIEW WITH SANDHYA RAO, former Editor, Tulika Books, Chennai

QUESTIONS TO EDITORS / PUBLISHERS

How is the publishing scenario with regard to books for children and young adults in India today?
It is very vibrant now. There's lots of publishing happening, some of it really good. The picture books segment is especially lively with work happening in many languages.

Environmental science is part of the curriculum of most schools and colleges. Still, light reading in the form of fiction helps inculcate values. Do you agree?

I think fiction is VERY important. Not just for inculcating values, but to fire the imagination because without imagination how do we make sense of our lives, the world, how do we live?

Do you think ecological wisdom can be imparted through fiction? Please state your opinion.

Certainly it can be. But it cannot be only through fiction. Remember, reality can be more amazing than fiction sometimes, so we have to understand the place that nonfiction has, the important role it plays.

Does your publishing house give importance to stories projecting ecological value – for example, depicting eco-friendly behavior, condemning environmentally unhealthy practices, the importance of biodiversity ,environmental pollution and other problems, dilemmas and solutions, etc.? If yes, please specify.

I have to clarify that I no longer work in Tulika Publishers. So, it would be good for you to contact Radhika Menon about this: **tulikabooks@vsnl.com**
However, having spent so many years doing children's books, and being still interested in it and writing, I will share my views. So I can say on behalf of Tulika that yes, it publishes very proactive books re ecology. If you check the website you will know: **www.tulikabooks.com**

Love of nature automatically creates awareness about the need for its conservation. Do the stories in your books have nature as a background?

If you're talking about my books, as in books I've written: yes, nature plays an important part. In fact at the core lies the belief that humans, animals, all of us are an integral part of one Nature. So, in Storm in the Garden, you have a snail's experience of rain and wind and so on. Another story talks about ants and suggests how they work so hard and go to many corners of their world having their adventures. My Friend the Sea is a story about the tsunami. And so on...

Are animals realistically and sensibly portrayed?

Absolutely true to their character... in the particular book concerned. When I write, they are true to their own characters as well as to the species. They may be quirky though, as in Crocodile Tears.

Is the traditional way of life, especially the lives of traditional people depicted in a positive manner?

Yes. But issues are not baulked from.

Do you have any special personal relationship with the natural environment?

Yes, I feel close to nature.

Illustrations are vital to children's books. How do you make use of illustrations to enhance the implicit message of your books?

Well, firstly, it's not so much message as the story. A good story told well, fiction or nonfiction, will carry a message even without it being spelled out. And in fact, spelling out a message does not make a good book. That said: certainly illustrations are vital. Word and picture go hand in hand.

Are your books eco-friendly? For example, do you use recycled paper?

Wish it were possible. It tends to be expensive.

Do you follow innovative practices in design to enhance you books? (for example, using traditional stylistic designs)

Using traditional designs is no longer innovative, everybody's doing it for everything, including for ads and cushion covers. The thing is create not simply copy. Certainly Tulika is very innovative.

What is your personal relationship with the natural environment? Do you follow eco-friendly practices in real life?

I practice what is possible. For instance, am careful how I use electricity. Don't use tissues. Don't pick flowers. Avoid toxic mosquito repellants. Things like that.

As a publisher, do you feel that ecology and the natural environment have found adequate and favourable representation in fiction for children and young adults in India?

Again, as I am not a publisher, I can answer this question only as an individual. No, I don't think there's adequate representation. It's only when it becomes a natural and seamless part of any narrative will it be adequately represented.

Can you further enlighten us/ give suggestions/comments/further experiences?

We are still at the teaching books stage. But certainly books in all the languages of India will make a substantial difference to children and the kind of adults they grow up to become. Reading and books help children grow into discerning adults, making informed decisions, helps keep them busy and calm at the same time....

Some Suggestions from Environmentalists

Interview with Payal B. Molur, Wildlife Educator, Bangalore

Me: Do you think children are aware of the ecological problems facing the world today?
Ms.Molur: The basic thing is knowing how to deal with population, which is the greatest problem, which creates food scarcity, waste, pollution, of course diseases. Everything is on the rise and everything these kids have to deal with. So I would hate for a child to jump into negativity. I would like the first ten years of the child to be positive about wildlife, not negative.
Me: Can you elaborate on that?
Ms.Molur: Our generation was outside all its time. I got to watch television when I was in Class 10 or 11. Our school bought one. We could not afford one. We spent a lot of time skipping, jumping, cycling, swimming. So I like the first ten years to be basically positive. I think because a lot of what you experience as a child is what takes you on in life. It gives a good feeling, if it is positive. So if I say " Oh, the frogs, so gorgeous and the frog is so helpful, it is really nice" to the child.You know, one of the problems that frogs face is when it is raining, they tend to go from pond to pond looking for their mates. They tend to cross the main roads. Cars

squash them. There is a simple solution. Instead of driving at 40 miles per hour, slow down to 15 or 20 miles per hour for that stretch of the forest. When I teach it to a child who is 10,11,12 years old, in story form, fiction, not fact, and then I throw in a little fact in between. Then I end in fact. "This gorgeous, so helpful Mr.Froggie goes to the doctor. Frogs are so cute, they go to the doctor." Next time she sees a frog on the road, the child thinks: " I must not squash it." She feels for the frog, she gets the message. My goal is that frogs should not be squashed, and this is achieved.

Me: Do you think environmental education that children get from textbooks is enough?

Ms.Molur: All our schools have Environmental Education. But unfortunately, from the few books I have seen (I can't confess I have seen all the books), I see that they talk about trains, coins, or domestic vs wild animals. So the point is that in Camford International, I teach grades 5 and 6. 10,11 and 12 approximately. So Camford's been really, really nice and allows me to follow my own curriculum. I made up my own curriculum. I have approximately 16 different curriculums that I have developed over time and made it based on Indian mentality. I must confess it was North Indian at first. Now it is more Coimbatore centric. So of course for Nagaland I have a different set of lessons. So I think it is extremely important. Reading is important, definitely.

Me: How far does the reading habit help shape children's attitudes?

Ms.Molur: I also do reading programmes, again for teacher training, not for children. My knowledge base is higher than the average person who does not read. Just the sheer grasping facility is higher, exposure is higher and personally I feel that tolerance is higher. In North India, they wonder, how do you live in the South? I know. I have exposure, Actually, I don't feel out of place since I have read about so many different cultures, people, lifestyles, perceptions about life. Nobody is right or wrong. There are so many different perspectives. What we react when we read about defines us. At the end of the day, what you feel about wildlife, people, culture- is what counts. What is everyone trying to do? Survive. Get food, clothing and shelter. Surivive. No matter what you are. Whether you are a frog, whether you are a mosquito, whether you are a human being, you must get these three basic things in life.

What you get from react broadening your scope through books? How should I have known about the world before the age of television unless I read books? My father was in the Air Force. I have travelled all over India. I had to keep changing friends every two years. So my friends were books. I was reading all the time. I have a lot of books upstairs. My husband is a wildlife scientist, a researcher. I am not a scientist, or a zoologist. I draw a lot of facts from him and I convert them into modules. He is into wildlife.

Me: A husband -wife team!
Ms.Molur: He keeps telling me things. It is good fun. It is useful. He says, "This is wrong. It should be like this." Fiction also. He has actually done a lot of work on and assessment and so on. He is one of the trustees of Zoooutreach He has been with them for 21 years. He is from Bangalore. There's Wildlife Institute of India, NCBS, Bangalore, Poona, Pondicherry. Wildlife photographers are here. They enjoy the joy of seeing something beautiful, the wonder. Photography can give you that.

Me: Can you tell me about illustrations?
Ms.Molur: There are very good illustrators in India. My book on Nagaland as illustrated by a Naga artist called Arjun. There are some really, really good illustrators.

This is absolutely mind-blowing book by Kenneth Opal, from the the *Silverwing* series. Absolutely mind-blowing because he bases his writing on facts, about how actual research on bats is done, silver-winged bats. It is narrated from the perspective of a bat. A researcher catches him and puts him into a cave, which is actually a cage. "What is this strange thing around my neck?" he asks himself. It is actually a radio collar. You can't hear bat's cries. But they have been recorded, fed to a computer and converted to the frequency that the human ear can hear. That is fac\scinating. How the fruit bat closes in on it's prey . . .

Ms.Molur (showing me a book): This is a turtle story. This lady Maya is one of the best illustrators of wildlife. It is amazing. But there are few like her. If there are, we don't know about them.

When I read, I would like the illustrations either to be cartoonish or to be scientifically correct even if it is an illustration. It is again about the subtle messages that the children get. If they are looking at the wrong picture, if they get the description wrong, even in fiction, it is with you. So the greatest thing about it is that the illustrations too are scientifically correct, even if it is a cartoon, you know, the colour, the expression, the face, everything will be really, really nice. This again is a story by Janaki Lenin She. came out with that King Cobra one (*King Cobra's Summer*). Pratham Books comes out with a lot of lively ones. So amazing. Yeah.

Ms.Molur (showing me another book): This one is not Indian but again fiction, someone else had given me from some other country. It is all about fish. And this is a series that the Wildlife Conservation Society came out with and again it is beautifully done. This is from the US. A series of 6,7. Or 8 books. Each one talks about different sea animals, coral reefs, but in a fiction form. There is a birthday party for different fish. How they react when an octopus comes. Something like that. It is realistic. From books one goes to movies and animation. You compare *Shark's Tale* and maybe *Happy Feet* and *Madagascar* as films. These are about animals which exist today. I absolutely hate *Madagascar*. I loved *Nemo*. I think it is one of the best animation movies about animals ever made. *Happy Feet* – kind of like it, kind of didn't. *Shark's Tale*, I really liked. The reason is, whether fish concerned or the animals were true to the character, what it is in the wild. Clamfish do like in sea anemones; they are slightly immune to the poison. And they do have to rub themselves on the anemone to ensure that they are immune to the anemone's ecretion. They talk about turtle migration. Then the shark comes. All the characters are presented correctly but in fiction. So I think it plays a big role in the children's perception of animals when they grow up and how they therefore treat the animal. A simple example - if I have to go to someone who has, hopefully, been through a workshop that I have conducted when he was a child and now, he is the CEO of Bosh and ask for donation for the conservation of animals. He will give a donation because he understands the implications- how it impacts conservation of the environment. Later, when a child grows up and is in a position, of a politician or perhaps a lawyer, his environmental knowledge will help society.

Me: What is the role of fiction in environmental conservation?
Ms.Molur: It plays a large role. It does change perception. Today, if I see an animal I can say what it is if I have read about it in a Gerald Durell book. The descriptions are fantastic and they stayed with me . right through. And I will tell you that. But if I have seen anything that is totally fiction, like *Happy Feet* or *The Elephant and the Ant*, I know nothing. I know a lot of people who think that orang-utans live here. Because it is in the book. It can give you wrong information. But there is no harm in doing that. What I am saying is that I wish both are taught. I would want *Jungle Book* to be there but at the same time having something that is also based on fact, taught. So if you have a reading club for children, and giving a whole month on wildlife books, you should have a discussion on how much is fact and how much is fiction. In our book, *Under the Canopy,* we have a section on folktales or culture. We have an entire hour. Do you think it is true? Do you think the author has ever seen a tiger in the wild? Very few people talk to kids like that, and ask their opinion and ideas or have a panel discussion for kids. Kids are always trying to feel grown up. "Creatie that creativity in the child" but also allow the child to understand the difference between fact and fiction. You do it in every other subject. Why not wildlife? Get the facts after they have the fun. Do anacondas, zebra, giraffe live in India? Ask children. They don't differentiate between continents. But hopefully, next year, after I do the course, they might tell their parents. Fiction is great. Enid Blyton portrays British wildlife, farming. Badgers and other countryside creatures.

Me: *Six Cousins at Mistletoe Farm?*
Ms.Molur: Other farm stories also. The Farm series.Flowers, trees, seasons, picnic, adventure, She [Blyton] was amazing.
Ms.Molur: I see a lot of difference. I see a friend of mine. Her daughter loves to read. So when I talk we can actually have an adult conversation. She is 13 years old. The other children of her age are not so knowledgeable. Again, it is the exposure that books give. She wins a lot of competitions, essay-writing, spelling bee..

And it is all because she is reading. In any language, aptitude in that language becomes much higher. Only three schools in Coimbatore do reading programmes. Camford International and Yellow Train are the ones I remember. They have fantastic reading programmes for parents and children.

Me: About children's books in India?

Ms.Molur: We have got some really good books. Again, it is parent exposure. Parents who are into reading buy books for their children. There are two good bookshops, Sapna and Connections. There is really a dearth of bookshops. I love bookshops, but they have only a small stock. Wildlife books are very poor. When I go specifically for wildlife books, we don't get them. We get omnibus of Jim Corbett, Kennth Andersen, foreign books, mostly. Durrell. Earlier, you couldn't get them. I used to go hunting in second-hand bookshops. There are a number of people writing about wildlife, especially about Indian wildlife.

Me: Deepak Dalal?

Payal: Also Janaki Lenin. Pratham publishes wildlife books. But otherwise no other publishers publish.

Me: Tulika and Katha have done a few.

Ms.Molur: Yes, I think *Under the Banyan*. Under the Neem. And there is the man who writes about the nuisance of monkeys in Delhi

Me: Ranjit Lal.

Ms.Molur: There are contemporary guys who have made books a lot of fun. I like his[Ranjit Lal's] writing. I wish more books would be written. Aagain, I don't know much about whether kids read Indian novels, I don't know. I know that, for example, in the schools I have visited, they have a good collection of books, but they have fantasy, fairy tales. Very few people have folktales.

Me: My students are mostly from rural backgrounds and they love folktales.

Ms.Molur: There are people who come and do storytelling sessions

Me: Like Geetha Ramanujam?

Ms.Molur: Hmm. .. You feel part of the book.

Me: Can you tell me about your work in Nagaland?

Ms.Molur: I go there once in three months. I coordinate with an NGO there. I teach children, especially the children of hunters, not to harm animals. There is a falcon which comes all the way from Africa. People kill it. Actually, it feeds on the locusts in Africa and thus helps to prevent famine there. I tell them that. Why did you choose subject? [Ecology and the Natural Environment]
Me: I think it is important.
Ms.Molur: I agree with you.

Me: Thank you!

INTERVIEW WITH 'OSAI'KALIDAS,
Coimbatore-based environmentalist

Q. Do you think story books will help environmental messages reach children?

OK: Story is the better way than a proverb which reaches quickly to the students arousing interest on the environment. Through stories we can feed students with ecology and ecosystem. They can learn about the existing animals, birds of the environment.

Q. What about the present curriculum and its concern to nature and environment?

OK: The present curriculum doesn't have any proper perception to our own environment and our region. It focuses and portrays only the western things and animals. For eg. The national animal of Tamilnadu is not known by the students here, but they learn about zebra, hippopotamus, giraffes which are not present in our eco system. This shows a lag in our school curriculum.

Q. Are there wild life organisation and wild life out reach which you are familiar with?

OK: WWF is a very good and active environmental organisation. Its volunteers are from Delhi. Persons like PayalMolur, Aanjai Varma, SalimWakar are some from Delhi. Mr. Jaganathan from Nature Conservation Society, Anaimalai; Mr. Ramji from Centre for Environment Education, Chennai were working on the environmental awareness to the school students. Then Mr. Raju, a retired teacher from Kotagiri, is working with the new curriculum for students.

Q. what is your opinion on the educational environment research from the literature books and curriculum?

OK: Yes, the researchers and the authors should provide good feel about environment curriculum.

In our curriculum there are environmental studies starting from UKG to12th Std. But, most of them are not related to our country's environment. It disappoints us. For example, the curriculum system shows the Western Ghats as negative picture like forest fire, poaching, deforestation, soil erosion. But, there are also positive visions. That positive side should be focussed successfully by portraying things like conservation of environment. This positive initiations should be focussed effectively and it helps to get an environmental awareness. The negative side which is presented in today's curriculum brings only the negative impact on the learners mind.

Q. What willyou prescribe and suggest the authors about environment?

OK: The understanding about nature should be observed in their writing by blending literature with aesthetic and ecology. The relationship between the environment and ecology should be given through the stories which will pave a good awareness to the environmental education along with literature.

The poems and rhymes of foreign nations for example, "Rain, rain go away!" poem is not suitable for our environmental context where on the contrary, we in our country are suffering from drought. The literature of past ancient periods focussed on the need and necessity of 'rain'. It should be inculcated and brought out as idea through the literature thus the westernised thoughts should be rid out and the culture of literature should be from our own environment. This should be promoted through curriculum.

If a writer writes a story, he should carry out the environmental surroundings in his work. For example, a man is sitting under a 'neem' tree, 'banyan' tree, birds like sparrow, eagle, etc., also the writer should describe about it features of leaves and fruits. This will inculcate the children's mind for ecology. This is only the author's perception, understanding and contribution to nature. By this kind of narrations in literature will develop the students' interest in ecology and environmental conservation from the interesting stories.

Q. what are your suggestions to the educationists in India for the development of wild life conservation?

OK: The Indian education system should promote the basic knowledge about nature to the students. It must give the exact distinctions of the wild animal's names with descriptions. Actually in India we don't have 'rabbit', only 'hare' is seen. There are lot of differences between rabbit and hare. Rabbit is in white colour and the hare looks brown with elongated ears. Likewise we don't have 'humming bird' we only have 'sun bird' in India. But in text books confuses the students as 'humming bird' is seen in our country. Also the animal 'Bison' is seen only in America we have 'Gaur'. Thus the educationists should avoid these confusions by illustrating proper distinctions of animals, and birds and plants which are existing in India.

The understanding about our environment and our species should be promoted through the literature. Thus this is the right medium to convey. Here the Indian s doesn't have keen ideology of our environment such as rivers, mountains and its origin and locations. This ideology about our own land should be encouraged and motivated through the school curriculum. It is the right and best way to conserve the environmental surroundings around us. The education system should be framed in a way to promote the conservation of nature and its resources. This is the need of the hour.

SR: Thank you, Sir!

About the Author

Dr. Shobha Ramaswamy

Dr.Shobha Ramaswamy, M.A, B.Ed., DCE.NET, M.Phil, PhD, is currently Professor of English at Karpagam Academy of Higher Education, Deemed-to-be- University, Coimbatore.She has more than 22 years of teaching experience in the field of English Literature and formerly headed the Department of English (Aided) at Kongunadu Arts and Science College, a College of Excellence. She is a research guide who has produced 11 PhDs and 14 M.Phils. She has also successfully completed a UGC Major Research Project on ecology in Indian literature for the young. Her areas of research interest are Archetypal and Mythological Cricitism, Ecocriticism, Travel Writing and Literature for children and young adults. She has published over 17 books and around 35 research papers.She is a reviewer for international journals based in the U.K. and Greece.She received the Dr.A.P.J. Abdul Kalam Professional Excellence Award in Theology from the University of Swahili, Panama. She has also written short stories and is an amateur artist and art therapist.

www.ingramcontent.com/pod-product-compliance
Lightning Source LLC
LaVergne TN
LVHW041844070526
838199LV00045BA/1428